proclamation 2

Aids for Interpreting the Lessons of the Church Year

holy week

Roy A. Harrisville
and
Charles D. Hackett

series b

editors: Elizabeth Achtemeier · Gerhard Krodel · Charles P. Price

FORTRESS PRESS PHILADELPHIA

Library of Congress Cataloging in Publication Data (Revised)

Main entry under title:

Proclamation 2.

Consists of 24 volumes in 3 series designated A, B, and C which correspond to the cycles of the three year lectionary plus 4 volumes covering the lesser festivals. Each series contains 8 basic volumes with the following titles: Advent-Christmas, Epiphany, Lent, Holy Week, Easter, Pentecost 1, Pentecost 2, and Pentecost 3.

CONTENTS: [etc.]—Series C: [1] Fuller, R. H. Advent-Christmas. [2] Pervo, R. I. and Carl III, W. J. Epiphany.—Thulin, R. L. et al. The lesser festivals. 4 v.

1. Bible—Homiletical use. 2. Bible—Liturgical lessons, English.

[BS534.5.P76] 251 79-7377

ISBN 0-8006-4079-9 (ser. C, v. 1)

9012F81 Printed in the United States of America 1-4086

Contents

Editor's Foreword

The commemoration of our Lord's last week was adopted by the church of Rome during the fifth or sixth century and quickly spread throughout Western Christendom. Prior to that time, some days of Holy Week had received special emphasis in different regions of the church. A female pilgrim with the probable name Egeria, while visiting sacred places in Egypt, the Holy Land, and Asia Minor described the Holy Week liturgy of Jerusalem during the late fourth or early fifth century (cf. G. Wilkinson, *Egeria's Travels* [London: SPCK, 1971]). Thus, for instance, on the afternoon of Palm Sunday a procession with palm branches moved from the Mount of Olives into Jerusalem commemorating Jesus' triumphal entry. The churches in Spain, Gaul, and England imitated this practice and had Palm Sunday processions which ended in the main church of a city. Maundy Thursday was the first weekday in Holy Week on which the Eucharist was celebrated in commemoration of the Last Supper. In the ancient church it served also as the occasion for the reconciliation of sinners. Its English name comes from the Latin *mandatum novum,* the "new commandment" of Jesus (John 13:34) which follows his washing of his disciples' feet. Good Friday in Egeria's time was the day of the veneration of the cross, a practice which continued in Jerusalem until the beginning of the seventh century when a Persian army conquered Jerusalem and took away the cross. By that time relics of the cross had made their way to the West and with them the rite of its veneration on Good Friday. Saturday in Holy Week marked the rest of Christ in the tomb and was a totally aliturgic day with a total fast. The Eucharist was not celebrated. The Saturday fast was followed by a vigil in which both the death and the resurrection of Christ were commemorated and which culminated as a joyful celebration of the Eucharist after midnight. In due course, the baptism of catechumens, the lighting of the paschal candle, and the blessing of the new fire were incorporated into this vigil.

The lessons for Holy Week, cycle B, are mainly from Isaiah, Hebrews, Mark, and John. The interpreters have endeavored to lead pastors into the appointed texts so that the word which once upon a time was spoken may resound anew today.

The exegete, Roy A. Harrisville, is Professor of New Testament at Luther Seminary, St. Paul, and author of many books, among them *The*

Concept of Newness in the New Testament (Minneapolis: Augsburg Publishing House,1960); *The Historical Jesus and the Kerygmatic Christ* (New York: Abingdon Press, 1964); *His Hidden Grace* (New York: Abingdon Press, 1965); *The Miracle of Mark* (Minneapolis: Augsburg Publishing House, 1967); *Commentary on Romans* (Minneapolis: Augsburg Publishing House, 1980); and *Benjamin Wisner Bacon, Pioneer in American Biblical Criticism* (Missoula, Mont.: Scholars Press, 1976).

The homiletician, Charles D. Hackett, is Assistant Professor of Church Ministries at Candler School of Theology, Emory University, in Atlanta, Georgia.

Gettysburg, Pa. GERHARD KRODEL

Sunday of the Passion
Palm Sunday

Lutheran	Roman Catholic	Episcopal	Pres/UCC/Chr	Meth/COCU
Zech. 9:9–10	Isa. 50:4–7	Isa. 45:21–25 or Isa. 52:13—53:12	Zech. 9:9–12	Zech. 9:9–12
Phil. 2:5–11	Phil. 2:6–11	Phil. 2:5–11	Heb. 12:1–6	Phil. 2:5–11
Mark 14:1—15:47 or Mark 15:1–39	Mark 14:1—15:47 or Mark 15:1–39	Mark (14:32–72) 15:1–39 (40–47)	Mark 11:1–11	Mark 14:1—15:47

EXEGESIS

First Lesson: Zech. 9:9–10. This passage in Zechariah is distinct from what precedes, both in form and in content. As to form, the third person is now exchanged for the second: "Rejoice greatly, O daughter of Zion!" and the entire address is fashioned after the herald's cry. As to content, in what precedes it is Yahweh who takes the land under his protection, and Israel is promised only a partial extension of its possessions; in these verses lordship is handed over to the Messiah, and Israel is promised world mastery. These verses, and the prophecy of Zechariah as a whole, originated in a period when Jerusalem had no king (cf. v. 9b: "Lo, your king comes to you"), the portrait of Messiah presumably reflecting the influence of Second Isaiah's fourth servant song (Isa. 52:13—53:12).

In v. 9 the "herald" is not a human messenger, but God himself. The reference to "your king" is to the king of the end time, of whom four statements are made. First, he is "righteous" (the RSV reads "triumphant"). The term "righteous" is to be construed in the passive sense and designates one who has received his right through a higher help, one to whom the divine righteousness has been given for his share. Since that "right" spells the salvation-creating righteousness of God, a connection thus is struck with the Messianic name in Jer. 23:6—"the Lord is our righteousness." Second, this king has been "helped" (the RSV reads "victorious"); in other words, he has behind him a period of distress. Solely by virtue of the divine grace and assistance, then, this king makes his entry. Third, he is "lowly" (the RSV reads "humble"), the reference being to his entry's lack of pomp. But there may also be a reminiscence here of the servant's form in Isaiah 53 ("he grew up before him like a young plant," v. 2; "we esteemed him stricken, smitten by God, and afflicted," v. 4; "he was oppressed, and he was afflicted, yet he opened not his mouth," v. 7). Fourth, this king comes "riding on an ass, on a colt the foal of an ass" (one, not two beasts are referred to, contra Matt. 21:2, 7, and the reason for this emphasis by repetition is to accent the purity of the line—an ass in contrast, say, to a mule). Contrast is immediately struck with the description which precedes, for the Messiah's mount is that of nobles, unless the author shares our modern devaluation of the beast and intends to express more concretely the lowliness of the rider. But noble or not, this king's riding is clearly for peace, as the following verse makes clear.

In v. 10 Yahweh declares that war will in the future no longer be a political means, and begins with the disarmament of his own people ("I will cut off the chariot from Ephraim and the war horse from Jerusalem; and the battle bow shall be cut off"). Further, this arbitrator-king will persuade the nations that war is no permanent solution ("he shall command peace to the nations"). What is promised, then, is a world mastery achieved by way of avoiding the engines of war, a mastery exercised by the Messiah who is supported by Yahweh and residing in Jerusalem.

From this description of the Messianic king and his reign two conclusions may be drawn. First, the portrait of Israel's salvation bringer has been vastly altered from the heroic figure of preexilic prophecy to the "justified" Messiah saved from the woes of the end time. Actually, Zechariah 9 may be a first attempt at combining Second Isaiah's servant and the royal deliverer of oldest Messianic tradition. Small wonder that the ancient Christian community expressly related this prophecy to Jesus (cf. Matt. 21:1–11 and John 12:12–19). Second, though riding for peace, the figure of the Messiah here is clearly political, and the prophecy is incapable of direct, unqualified application to Jesus of Nazareth (note the omission of v. 10 in Matthew 21 and John 12). However eschatological the mood, the political limit remains.

Second Lesson: Heb. 12:1–6. Writing from Alexandria to a community weary with waiting for Christ's return, in a language and conceptuality highly reminiscent of the Gnostic myth, the author of Hebrews in 12:1–6 adapts a portion of the community's confession to the theme of discipleship. Drawn by a vision of the future, and thus reflecting the dialectic of faith as a reaching for what is already given—a feature dominating the entire Epistle—the verses begin with a reference to the "cloud of witnesses" who have met the goal of their "wandering" and now observe the community's "race" through the zone of battle and death. How this race comes to be such is made clear in v. 1, in which the community is described as burdened with a "weight" laid on it by the "sin which clings so closely," a weight consisting of the visible with its charms or the threat of persecution. Faith, then, is marked by "perseverance" in the race (corresponding to the "struggle" in 12:4 which derives from the same root, and the "discipline" in 12:5–11), that is, by holding the original "assurance" (11:1) firm to the end—perhaps a shift in understanding over against Paul's summons to the "obedience of faith."

Since for the author of Hebrews mere admonition does not suffice, he attempts to strengthen the community by illustrating in v. 2 with the example of Christ himself the necessity of discipleship. It would be an error, however, to construe the illustration in purely ethical fashion, or to read it in terms of Jesus' own "moral development," since Jesus is here portrayed not merely as Pioneer of the community's faith—through his own experience conscious of its weakness and thus of its temptation to weariness—but also as Perfecter.

The word "perfecter" has a twofold signification. First, Jesus Christ, the great High Priest by whose death the fallen creation is redeemed, in whom all things will ultimately come to rest, draws his community after him toward its goal. Second, insofar as Christ's sacrifice has already created participation in his own "fulfillment"—a participation already enjoyed in this life (cf. 12:22–24)—the goal toward which the community advances is not hidden, nor is the "race" in doubt. The illustration thus reflects that "eschatological dialectic" which also marks the Epistle as a whole, and which finally distances our author from the myth which he employs as vehicle. Just as the myth, the author of Hebrews can speak of a heavenly goal, of "weights" which hinder the faithful, and of believing existence as a procession characterized by suffering. He too can speak of a Redeemer who is divine in origin and nonetheless like his "brethren." He can even speak of that Redeemer's putting aside his "flesh" in an ascent toward God. At the heart and core of his gospel, however, is the confession that participation in the Redeemer's redemption or the completion of the race occurs solely by virtue of an altogether historical, once-for-all event—the death of Jesus of Nazareth.

It may well be that the NT tends to avoid describing faith as discipleship—for fear of endangering the qualitative difference between Christ and his own. It may well be that this pericope is not firmly anchored in the whole of the Epistle. But from the perspective of the whole, the proper exposition of our verses lies in 2:10: "For it was fitting that he, for whom and by whom all things exist, in bringing many sons to glory, should make the pioneer of their salvation perfect through suffering." The "pioneering" is thus interpreted by the "perfecting," by the suffering, by Jesus' sacrifice of his own body and blood.

Gospel: Mark 14:1—15:47. Mark 14:1 begins the oldest record of Jesus' passion, and perhaps also the oldest portion of the entire Gospel tradition. Prior to the Gospels' assuming written form, when the tradition was transmitted orally, this record may have had its birth in the worship of the earliest Christian community. For example, the Supper narrative in 14:22–24 and references to the days of Passover week in 14:1, 12, 17 and 15:1, 42 may reflect the communion practice and anniversary observation of Jesus' death in the community for which Mark wrote. In its present shape the narrative no doubt differs greatly from its oral antecedents. Whether by Mark or his predecessors, narrative, reflection, apologetic, and other materials have been added, stimulated by a host of occasions in the community's life.

The chapters reach their culmination in the historical reference in 15:26 ("And the inscription of the charge against him read, 'The king of the Jews' "), in Jesus' cry from the cross in 15:34 ("My God, my God, why hast thou forsaken me?"), and in the confession of the centurion in 15:39 ("Truly this man was the Son of God!"). Mark's intention is thus to declare that what occurs in Jesus' dereliction is his exaltation and the ushering in of the end time.

What is striking is that Mark's story is told largely in the language of the OT. The term "betray" or "deliver" (in 14:10–11, 18, 21, 41–42, 44 and 15:1) is the same used in the Septuagint version of Isaiah's fourth servant song (Isa. 53:6). The reference to Jesus' silence before Pilate is reminiscent of Ps. 38:12–14 or Isa. 53:7. The soldiers' mocking in 15:16–20 is reported after the style of the mistreatment of the servant in Isaiah 50 and 53. The offering of wine mingled with myrrh contains an allusion to Prov. 31:6–7. The division of garments renders in indirect discourse the psalmist's complaint in Ps. 22:18; Jesus' crucifixion between the two thieves hides a reminiscence of Isa. 53:12 and 27; and the Septuagint translation of Lam. 2:15, Pss. 22:6–7, 69:9, and 109:25 contains the same verbs which appear in Mark 15:29 and 32. Finally, Jesus' cry is just short of a literal repetition of Ps. 22:1, and the sponge filled with vinegar in 15:36 sets in indirect speech the psalmist's lament in Ps. 69:21.

These references, reminiscences, and allusions reflect a fundamental conviction threading throughout the entire Gospel: The word of God gives integrity to the event. In other words, Mark does not observe the circumstances of Jesus' death, exclaim, "Aha! The very same things were predicted in the Old Testament!'' and then proceed to prove the truth of the OT word by the contemporary event, or vice versa. Mark rather conceives the OT word, or better, the God whose activity is announced in it, as constitutive of the life and destiny of Jesus. For this reason, the Son of man ''must suffer many things'' (8:31), ''as it is written of him'' (14:21). For the centurion, of course, it is Jesus' loud cry and death which convince him that ''this man was the Son of God,'' and Mark's purpose is thus to preach that only in his death can Jesus be rightly seen as God's Son. But however appropriate the centurion's confession—the only instance in Mark in which a human says such a thing about Jesus—the distance between him and the evangelist remains. To the Gentile, ''Son of God'' denotes a special human being with divine powers, be it a philosopher or a Caesar or a miracle worker. Further, for the centurion, it is *because Jesus dies* that he is acknowledged to be Son of God. For Mark, on the other hand, it is *because Jesus is God's Son*—because God is author of the Gospel event which is Jesus Christ, Son of God—that he dies. Nevertheless, the centurion penetrates the secret of Jesus' identity, a secret drawn by Mark over the entirety of Jesus' career and till now known only to the demons. And because that secret is extended to Jesus' life and career, it is necessary to revise the old dictum according to which the Gospel of Mark (indeed every New Testament Gospel) is in essence a passion narrative with a rather lengthy introduction. The Gospel throughout is a ''book of secret epiphanies.''

There are themes which are common to the three texts and might explain their being clustered together. First, each text implies that God is the initiator of the events described. The Yahweh of Zechariah heralds the arrival of the royal servant because it is he who sends the servant to Zion; in Hebrews the future is already disclosed to the community because God has shown himself in the sacrifice of Christ, and in Mark Jesus suffers because he ''must,'' because God is author of the event. Second, the motif of suffering is common to all three: Zechariah's royal Messiah-servant has been ''helped'' through a period of trial; Hebrews' ''pioneer and perfecter'' is such by virtue of his high-priestly sacrifice, and the identity of Mark's Jesus is disclosed in his death. Third, all three texts are universal in scope: in Zechariah Messiah's dominion is ''from sea to sea,'' and at issue in Hebrews and Mark is a contention regarding world history—the redemption of all creation occurs in Jesus' death.

It is not possible, of course, simply to trace an arc from Zechariah to Mark and Hebrews. They are distinguished not only by their form (in Zechariah prophecy, in Mark narrative-proclamation, in Hebrews homology) and by the persons addressed (Israel, any and all readers or hearers, the community of believers), but above all by a vast interval of time. Zechariah cannot view the Messiah-servant's suffering as the eschatological deed par excellence, and thus cannot share the dialectic according to which the faithful are assured of the future by virtue of what they have already received. For Zechariah the political limit remains.

HOMILETICAL INTERPRETATION

In coming to the Palm Sunday lections, the preacher is coming to the beginning of that liturgical sequence which is at the heart of the church's life. This day begins the sequence of Holy Week and Easter which embodies the earliest kerygma and provides the yearly opportunity for us to experience and appropriate the paschal mystery.

Therefore it is doubly important for the preacher to have in mind the whole sweep of the paschal drama as he or she approaches any one set of readings. In a period of six liturgical days, Jesus will enter Jerusalem in apparent triumph and be betrayed, isolated, tortured, and killed. On the seventh day there will be a cosmic rest paradoxically corresponding to the Sabbath day of rest observed by God in the first creation. Then, on Easter Sunday, beginning with an evening vigil which moves from the darkness of night and death to the morning of life and light, the church proclaims the empty tomb, the resurrection, and re-creation. At least from the time of Hippolytus in the early third century, this was the night in which new Christians were baptized so as to signify their union with the Lord in his dying and rising. In this the early church was elaborating a theological key in Paul: "We were buried therefore with him by baptism into death, so that as Christ was raised from the dead by the glory of the Father, we too might walk in newness of life. For if we have been united with him in a death like his, we shall certainly be united with him in a resurrection like his" (Rom. 6:4–5).

Thus any adequate interpretation of the Holy Week readings must understand them in a framework of participation. This foundational Christian story is told from Palm Sunday through Easter. In its measured telling we are asked to find ourselves, our own world, and our own lives. The offer of Holy Week and Easter is victory over the powers of sin, evil, and death. Such power, however, comes only by the cross. The aim of the paschal cycle is our participation in Jesus' death and resurrection to the end that our own death might eventuate in divine re-creation.

The First Lesson is signal for the beginning of this paschal cycle. It is the prophecy on which is built the meaning of Jesus' entry into Jerusalem, the event which gives this day its name. Palm Sunday church services which do not begin with a biblical account of Jesus' entry into the Holy City (usually Matt. 21:1–11, Mark 11:1–11a, or Luke 19:29–40, depending on the lectionary cycle) have particular need for the Zechariah lesson. Services which *do* begin with a re-creation of Jesus' triumphal entry into the city have need of this prophecy in order to tie the principal liturgical action, the entry, to the long reading of the Marcan passion narrative which constitutes the Gospel and in turn leads Palm Sunday into the solemn downward movement toward Good Friday.

Zechariah's "king" who comes to Zion is the longed-for Messiah. He is thus anointed to rule—that is, to make righteous judgments—as were the judges, David, and Solomon. He is of the royal line, and so he rides a young purebred male beast: "an ass" which is "a colt the foal of an ass."

Moreover, the Messiah comes as a bringer of peace. His manner of entry, though symbolically pure and royal, is not at the head of an army. He shall break the battle bow and shall say shalom (peace, wholeness, harmony) to all people.

This much the early church could easily find to have been a foretelling of Jesus. But the expectation of Zechariah, and clearly of the Hebrew people, was for a political Messiah. This would be a Messiah who would deliver Israel from its years of bondage to foreign conquerors. Thus the promise of Zechariah for a Jew of Jesus' time was for a Messiah who would drive out the hated Romans and establish Jewish sovereignty and prosperity. Some of Jesus' contemporaries believed that this Messiah would be primarily political and military (for example, the Zealots), while others had a more supernaturalistic conception of the Messiah's action (for example, the people of Qumran). In all cases, however, the mark of the Messiah would be his success in freeing God's people from their slavery and establishing a peaceful order based in Jerusalem and covering the whole world, even "to the ends of the earth." This part of the prophecy was a problem and an opportunity for the post-Easter church. As such it provides the structure for the whole paschal hermeneutic. From the Christian point of view Jesus fulfilled the prophecy, but the power of sin prevented the people from recognizing his Messiahship. Thus we have the irony of Palm Sunday. Jesus enters the city and is hailed as Messiah. In greeting him thus, the people are doing the right thing for the wrong reason. They expect him to overthrow Caesar. Their anger, their wish for vengeance, their preoccupation with political and economic power blind them to the truth of who is among them. They cannot see beyond their own expectations. They will be instrumental in killing their own King! (Mark 15:12–15).

It is a sense of this irony which provides a preacher with a purchase on the contemporary human situation. As a world population, as a nation, as special interest groups, and as individuals, we all continue in our fear and anger to want to seize power, identify the enemies, and destroy them. Each of us seeks to control his or her own destiny. The more we do, the more anxious we become as individuals and the more arrogant and dangerous we become as groups or as a nation. The more we tend, in our frustration and fear, to see God's will as identical with how we want our problems solved, the more we fit the tragic irony of those who hailed Jesus as the Messiah on Palm Sunday but turned angry and violent when he did not behave as they supposed he should.

It is at this point that the narrative irony of the Palm Sunday story is conjoined with the universal human irony which we call sin. In this context the axiom that Jesus died for our sins—not ours only but the sins of the whole world—takes on yet another level of meaning. This is the cosmic irony turned upside down. God conquered the power of sin not by opposing it on its own terms but precisely by submitting to it. It is to this that both the Second Lesson and the Gospel for Palm Sunday speak, each in its own way.

The first six verses of the twelfth chapter of Hebrews move us away from narrative to theological reflection. The author, writing self-consciously to believers, attempts to support his community in times of trial and difficulty. Jesus has not returned yet and the church is asking why. Christians are tempted and persecuted, and at least some are defecting. Again, the church is asking why.

In his Neoplatonic fashion, the author of Hebrews suggests a version of the great paschal mystery of participation which we have already found in Paul and delineated in the sweep of the Holy Week–Easter liturgy. Jesus, the preexistent High Priest, has come down from the heavenly realm and has entered into our human situation. In fact, Jesus endured the same effects of sin which we human beings experience—temptation and fear. When Jesus endured the death of the cross, he submitted himself to the worst that we humans can be subjected to. In so doing he became our Pioneer, that is, the one who goes through fearful and uncharted places so that when we enter them ourselves we know at least that someone has been there before us, and our experience will not be utter isolation.

But Jesus was more than a pioneer. The author says that *by* his pioneering Jesus became the Author and Finisher of our faith. This is to say that by submitting to the effects of sin and enduring the worst that the powers of death could do, Jesus became available to us in a special way. He was designated, through the Easter resurrection, the one who is available to us and through whom we can find the strength to endure; we can endure the effects of sin because he has submitted and has in turn been elevated to the symbolic place of majesty and victory—the right hand of the throne of God. Thus the author finds again, within the framework of his gnostically oriented hermeneutic, the Pauline insight that because Jesus has died our death and been raised, we who must die can share in his resurrection.

So from the ironic narrative of Jesus' triumphal entry into Jerusalem the readings move us through a brief reflection on the purpose of Jesus' sufferings to the Marcan story of the passion. Here is the story told from Wednesday in Holy Week through Good Friday. It begins with the conspiracy of the high priests to have him done away with and continues through the Last Supper, the vigil in the garden, the arrest, the trial, the suffering, and the death and burial.

Inasmuch as it is the heart of the kerygma and is in fact probably the oldest continuous narrative in the Christian tradition, it is almost too rich to preach. We are tempted to take this or that portion of the story and develop a sermon of more limited scope. Thus a sermon on the chief priests and the temptations of power, or a sermon on the woman who anoints Jesus and the issue of good practical works versus beautiful holy gestures, tempts us. This is Palm Sunday, however, and such temptations are better delayed until later in the year. The long line of Sundays after Pentecost will provide the chances for more limited homiletical focus. Today the preacher's job is to find the thread of the Marcan passion narrative and interface it with the Palm Sunday irony and the contemporary human experience of sin and death. In so seeking, we find that Mark was made for Holy Week and Holy Week for his theology.

If we follow the intention of this oldest but very subtly constructed Gospel, we find that there is an inverse relationship between the actual power which Jesus exercises and the sphere of creation which recognizes his identity as Son of God. At the beginning of the Gospel, Jesus is baptized but he and he *alone* sees the spirit descend and hears the voice designating him as Son (Mark 1:9ff.). He then goes to the wilderness where he is recognized by Satan and angels. He returns to begin his ministry, and though he speaks with authority, human beings do not identify him. Significantly, however, the unclean spirits do (Mark 1:24). In other words, at the beginning phase of Jesus' ministry, he displays great power but is recognized only by representatives of the supernatural.

At precisely the halfway point in the Gospel (if we excise the so-called little apocalypse, Mark 13:5–37), Peter makes his confession and Jesus is identified as Son of God before Peter and his identity is disclosed symbolically to both Jews and the founder of the church (Mark 9:7). From this point on, Jesus' power is less and less triumphant. He is on his way to Jerusalem to suffer. From his entry on Palm Sunday, the intensity of the conflict and misunderstanding—the tragic irony of the Palm Sunday liturgy—escalates. Finally, misperceived by the people to whom he was sent, ironically designated King of the Jews by the gentile governor Pilate (Mark 15:26), Jesus is crucified. In utter humiliation and agony he dies. Mark's Jesus does not, like Matthew's, yield up his spirit (Matt. 27:50). After crying out the agony of utter abandonment, "My God, my God, why have you forsaken me?" (Mark 15:34 NAB), Jesus simply breathes his last (Mark 15:37). The utter finality of breathing his last leaves no doubt as to his status: he is dead; he is no more. At this point the gentile centurion who stood facing him and *saw* that he "breathed his last" identified him on behalf of the pagan, gentile world: "Truly this man was the Son of God" (Mark 15:39).

From the beginning Jesus was *ontologically* the Son of God. Despite this, however, his *functionality* as Savior, that is, as the one who could defeat the powers of sin and death as they operated in and among human beings, depended on his being *recognized* for who he was. With puzzling and almost perverse consistency, Mark's Jesus keeps his identity a "secret"; he consistently forbids those whom he has helped to tell of him. His true identity must apparently be manifest only in and through his abandoned, powerless death. The irony of Palm Sunday now meets the paradox of Mark's theology. All of us look for a savior. We envision this savior much as the Jews looked for a Messiah. But the savior does not save us from death; instead he comes and dies exactly the death each of us will die. And mysteriously, it is only in the powerless dying that we are given power to appropriate our own deaths as salvific and not merely as destructive.

Thus the three readings which begin Holy Week and Easter hang together on the strong thread of our own experience of sin and death. We look for a way out. There is no way out; there is only the way through. Jesus has deigned to come among us and has taken upon himself what we all must go through. In this the titles coalesce: Messiah, Pioneer, and Son of God. These he is because he is one of us: subject to sin and death, powerless, and human.

Monday in Holy Week

Lutheran	Roman Catholic	Episcopal	Pres/UCC/Chr	Meth/COCU
Isa. 42:1–9	Isa. 42:1–7	Isa. 42:1–9	Isa. 50:4–10	Isa. 42:1–9
Heb. 9:11–15		Heb. 11:39—12:3	Heb. 9:11–15	Heb. 9:11–15
John 12:1–11	John 12:1–11	John 12:1–11 or Mark 14:3–9	Luke 19:41–48	John 12:1–11

EXEGESIS

First Lesson: Isa. 42:1–9. This passage was penned at Babylon, within a period of the Exile marked by the successes of the Persian king Cyrus. It combines the first servant song (vv. 1–4), which portrays the appointment and task of that mysterious and hotly disputed figure, with the fragment of a "Cyrus song." The author appears to have spliced these songs into his text after he had first written his prophecy, particularly since the portrait of the servant does not easily suit his message. The style is hymnic, reminiscent of the Psalter, allowing the inference that the prophet wove types and themes belonging to Israel's worship into his message.

The servant song, reminiscent of the designation of a king, first refers to the servant's "credentials," to the approval and support of God who equips him for his task. The opening words in v. 1 are thus determinative for the whole: "Behold my servant!" The clauses which immediately follow are synonymous and accent God's favor toward his servant ("whom I uphold . . . in whom my soul delights"). In v. 1bff. the *task* of the servant is described in threefold fashion, and in each instance by way of the term "justice": The servant will make known the new ordering of the world beginning with the victories of Cyrus ("he will bring forth justice to the nations," v. 1b); his task will achieve its goal ("he will faithfully bring forth justice"—the word translated "faithfully" actually means "in reality," v. 3b); and his work will end in the decision that the claims of the heathen gods are declared to be nothing ("establish justice in the earth," v. 4b). The *manner* in which the servant is to execute his task is then described in negative clauses: His manner of gaining attention will be vastly different from that of earlier prophets ("he will not cry or lift up his voice, or make it heard in the street," v. 2); his activity will contradict the hard law of the world that the broken and smoldering must die ("A bruised reed he will not break . . . a dimly burning wick he will not quench,'' v. 3a; is the reference to the mood of his people going into exile?); and though led into severe suffering (resistance from his own people?), the servant will not halt his work (''he will not fail or be discouraged,'' v. 4a). The song then concludes with the statement that the servant's message corresponds to the nations' yearning for rescue (''the coastlands wait for his law,'' v. 4b).

In the Cyrus song, addressed to doubts that a heathen king can be Yahweh's tool for world history or Israel's destiny, the first verse (v. 5) yields the point of departure and states a truth which can reckon on universal assent: Yahweh is ''God the Father Almighty, maker of heaven and earth.'' Yahweh is engaged in a continual creating—''he gives breath to the people upon [earth] and spirit to those who walk in it.'' V. 6a then states the king's credentials: ''I have called you . . . have taken you by the hand and kept you.'' The following verses state the meaning of Cyrus's task: In v. 6b he is given as an ''obligation to the people'' (the RSV translation ''covenant'' derives from a secondary usage of the original term), and as a ''light to the nations.'' That is, he is the personal warranty of the people's rescue. V. 7 then states the goal of the king's task: he is obliged to bring to the world the order intended by Yahweh, to create the physical or political basis upon which the nations may exist in peace and freedom—''to open the eyes that are blind, to bring out the prisoners.'' The song concludes with Yahweh's assertion—''I am the Lord . . . my glory I give to no other''—followed by the declaration that his first prophecies respecting the previous successes of the Persian monarch came true (''Behold!''), and with the promise of a new creation—Israel's and the nations' coming rescue.

Second Lesson: Heb. 9:11–15. Christ is described in this passage as ''great high priest'' (cf. 2:17; 3:1; 4:14–15; 5:5, 10; 6:20; 7:26; 8:1, 3) and ''mediator of a new covenant'' and again in language strange to the remainder of the NT. The contrast between the earthly and heavenly worlds, drawn in the distinction between the ''tent'' or tabernacle ''made with hands'' and that which is ''not of this creation'' (v. 11), between the ''purification of the flesh'' through the sacrifices of the ancient cultus and the purification of conscience ''through the eternal Spirit'' (vv. 13–14), seems to reflect the uncritical appropriation of a mythical idea. But again, the similarity between Hebrews and mythological speculation is outweighed by the dissimilarity. That ''tent'' through which Jesus passes is not a mere model of the earthly tabernacle. The ''tent'' is Jesus' own earthly, historical existence culminating in his death—elsewhere referred to as his ''flesh'' (cf. 10:20). Thus the death in which Christ offers himself to God is both the ''hindrance'' or veil before the heavenly world, the Holy Place, *and* the entry into that world. It is the death which yields the content and high point of Christ's high-priestly activity. However dependent upon the language and conceptuality of the myth, Hebrews conceives the history of the Christian community as beginning not with a metaphysical state or mythical idea but historically—with Golgotha. Only where Jesus' "flesh" is understood as an exponent of the material world, as earthly and historical, can sense be made of the statement that taking his blood he penetrated to the Holy Place and secured access on behalf of his own.

In. vv. 13–14, the author makes clear that the contrast between the purifications achieved by the earthly and heavenly sanctuaries is created by the "blood of Christ." In the former, purification had to do merely with the flesh. The "consciousness of sin" (10:2), knowledge of the distance between oneself and God, persisted. Such consciousness may drive to exertion, to an attempt to bridge the distance, but since such exertion aims only at a purification of the flesh, it cannot annul the "bad conscience"—the exertion remains a "dead work" (v. 14). The effect of Jesus' high-priestly activity, on the other hand, consists in the purification of conscience, and thus makes possible a genuine service to God.

It is for this reason, the author writes, that Jesus is "mediator of a new covenant." It is often stated that the term translated "covenant" implies a pact between parties of unequal rank, with the exception of 9:16–17, in which the term is used only in a legal sense and translated "testament." But according to Hebrews, activity on the part of those with whom God establishes his "covenant" begins only *after* that covenant is made. For this reason the word "covenant" as commonly used is inadequate to express the full force of a term which marks an arrangement initiated by God concerning that which is his. The sphere of *revelation* is thus the proper locus of "covenant." By referring to the "new covenant," the author of Hebrews makes clear that this arrangement established by means of Jesus' sacrificial death is an eschatological arrangement, that is, an ordering of the divine relationship to humanity in a way never to be supplanted or surpassed (this is also the force of the term for "new" in the Supper narratives of Luke and 1 Corinthians; cf. Luke 22:20 and 1 Cor. 11:25). And this was Israel's hope, voiced in the promise of Jer. 31:31ff.

Finally, this "covenant" made through Christ's death is the presupposition for the reception of the "promised eternal inheritance" (or, better, "the promise of the eternal inheritance"), the term "inheritance" to be construed less in a juridical than in a local sense, as a "taking possession of the land," as entry into the heavenly world (v. 15).

It is clear to the author of Hebrews that Christ is the "end" not only of the "myth," reflected in the writer's language and conceptuality, but the end of the law as well, typified in the earthly sanctuary and its cultus.

The historical sacrifice of Christ as hindrance and as access, as transcending a mere fleshly cleansing in a purification of conscience for service to the living God, is the answer to both Jew and Greek, but by way of the fracture of both Jewish law and Greek myth.

Gospel: Mark 14:3–9. Until recently, it has been customary to treat the pericope in Mark 14:3–9 as a "paradigm" or "apothegm," in which an action furnishes the framework for a word of Jesus. In the opinion of the majority, however, the word of Jesus in vv. 7–9 which transfigures the woman's deed into a prophetic sign ("she has anointed my body beforehand for burying," v. 8) is not an original part of the story but was added later for the purpose of including the episode in the passion narrative. In its present form, the pericope is thus a biographical legend. Originally, the scene culminated in Jesus' praise of the woman's deed as a "beautiful thing," in contrast to the usual practice of almsgiving. It may thus be easily excerpted from chap. 14 without damage to the context. Support for such a contention is drawn from the fact that though Matthew includes this scene at approximately the same place in his passion story, Luke sets it in an entirely different context (cf. Luke 7:36ff.), where it serves as framework for Jesus' conversation with Simon, now identified as a Pharisee. The fourth evangelist likewise includes the story but in contrast to Mark fixes its occurrence "six days before the Passover" (John 12:1).

It is highly probable that this pericope enjoyed independent circulation prior to its incorporation in the written Gospels—Mark's more or less stylized introduction ("and while he was at Bethany," v. 1) appears to support that notion—though the optimism of an earlier generation regarding the scholar's ability to separate what an evangelist inherited from what the evangelist *did* with what he inherited was often extreme. But the conclusion drawn by the majority to the effect that this story may be removed from the passion history without doing violence to the context rests on a serious misapprehension of Mark's purpose.

The strange and unusual features of the story, so often overlooked in exposition, are a clue to the evangelist's aim. The company at table appears to be composed not only of Jesus' friends and followers but also of his enemies, represented in the word of indignation in v. 4 ("there were some who said to themselves indignantly, 'Why was the ointment thus wasted?' "). The anointing takes place at an ordinary table fellowship—contrary to usual custom. There were anointings aplenty, but they occurred at times of special celebration, at marriage feasts, for example, when oil was dripped on the head of the bride in such fashion as to indicate she was either a widow or a virgin. Here there is no reference to a special occasion—a woman invades a table fellowship apparently designed only for men and performs an act out of all proportion to the event. The oil, kept in an alabaster container, consisted of a distillation which only the rich could afford ("pure nard, very costly," v. 3), its value inconceivably high—enough to pay three hundred persons a day's wage, if the parable in Matthew 20 yields any indication (cf. Matt. 20:2).

These curious features conspire to suggest something infinitely more than a mere symbolizing of the idea that social obligations must at times give way to religious obligations, or that a spontaneous proof of personal love is more important than diminishing poverty. While it is true that the needy will never disappear, that thus the hand of the pious may always be open ("you always have the poor with you, and whenever you will, you can do good to them," v. 7; cf. Deut. 15:11), in Scripture the social obligation or diminution of poverty is never regarded as optional. What renders such activity optional *in this case,* and thus marks the woman's action as worthy of everlasting remembrance ("wherever the gospel is preached in the whole world, what she has done will be told in memory of her," v. 9), is that she has anointed the Messiah—the more costly the oil, the greater the honor. In Mark's Gospel, this act marks the commencement of the passion—the one about to go to his death is the Anointed One. The scene is thus integral to the narrative. In harmony with the veil of secrecy which the evangelist draws over all of Jesus' career, the action is misunderstood—the onlookers perceive nothing but a waste of precious stuff—not least by later tradition which was more concerned with identifying Jesus' host or naming the woman (cf. Luke 7:36 and John 12:3) than with the significance of the action itself.

"Behold my servant!"—not now, as with Second Isaiah, installed before a royal or even celestial company, but in hiddenness and imperceptibility; not now appointed to political or martial success, and in such fashion to effect a recognizably new ordering of the world, but appointed to misunderstanding and death, a Messiah for whom resistance is not merely implied ("he will not fail or be discouraged," Isa. 42:4) but furnishes the core and culmination of his career. For his law, indeed, "the coastlands wait" (Isa. 42:4), but that law is the law of "the new covenant," in which "the hopes and fears of all the years" are met in such fashion as to transcend and therefore fracture them—a covenant spelling an end to myth and law, a covenant rooted in the death of Jesus of Nazareth, Mark's "secret Messiah."

HOMILETICAL INTERPRETATION

Monday in Holy Week carries forward toward Good Friday the ironic theme of cosmic misunderstanding which is at the heart of Palm Sunday.

The First Lesson, alluded to in the Song of Simeon (Luke 2:22ff.), has christological significance for the church. The Messiah is described as being given the power from almighty God to exercise judgment over all people. This judgment is to be understood in the OT sense of establishing a wise and peaceful order which is righteous, that is, in accordance with God's will. Moreover, Messiah shall establish this reign of God not with the conventional means of warfare and terror, but with patience, perseverance, and gentleness. The reign which will result will be a state of human society—and perhaps a state of nature—so transformed that the blind will see and those who are in prison can be released. In other words, the Messiah will inaugurate the Kingdom of God in which there will be harmony, peace, health, and joy because at last everything will conform to the law of God.

In retrospect, Jesus seems to have fulfilled exactly what was new, unexpected, and radical in this prophecy. He was above all gentle, loving, and patient, providing these words are not understood in a sentimental manner. Moreover, he came proclaiming by word and deed the arrival of a Kingdom of God which was characterized by peace, wholeness, freedom, and joy. Obviously, however, this raises a problem because Jesus was not recognized as Messiah by those of his time. In fact, he was reviled and killed. Moreover, his life and death did not and have not seemed to bring about the reign of peace and joy of which the prophet speaks. It is at this point that the preacher finds an existential interface with the contemporary situation. The death of Jesus has not ushered in anything like the Kingdom of God of OT prophecy and first-century expectation. Moreover, the ideals and virtues of justice, peace, patience, and gentleness seem, even to the extent we are able to approximate them, to come to naught. We are not often able to discern or sustain them, and even when we do, it turns out that even the best intentions become distorted and produce unexpected, destructive results. On a social level, the road to the tragedy of Vietnam was paved with good intentions. On a personal level, we enter marriages with the best intentions of making one another fulfilled and happy. The divorce statistics witness to the rate at which this undertaking goes awry. Jesus seems to have been the One prophesied to bring the kingdom of wholeness and joy. He lived and was crucified and died, and the world seems no different for his having been here. We still live, as Paul would put it, in a world where we do not even understand our own actions, where with the best intentions on the part of individuals and social structures we still wind up doing not the things we wanted to do but precisely those things we did not want to do. Our social service programs tend to produce anger and frustration rather than improving human life. Our individual gestures of kindness and good will wind up hurting others or causing misunderstandings. We still live in a world in which sin, however we conceive that power, reigns unabated.

Today's Second Lesson and Gospel offer two different answers for this dilemma.

The author of Hebrews uses the cultic and mythological imagery of both the Hellenistic and Hebrew worlds to suggest that, in fact, Jesus' life and death have already made the crucial difference in human existence in that we are free from the ongoing effects of sin. The mythic formulation is that Jesus, being a sinless and divine being, became one of us and suffered the inevitable effects of the sinful human condition—death. By his willingness to take on the human condition, Jesus fulfilled completely the function which cultic sacrifice could only approximate; he removed the stain of past sin and interrupted its continuing effect in human life. Realizing that sin was continuing to have its baleful effect, the author of Hebrews suggests all three of the alternatives which Christian theology has chosen to explain why sin continues to reign even after it has been overcome by Jesus: (1) the promise has been essentially fulfilled, but its completion awaits the Parousia; (2) the promise has been fulfilled, and we will find this is true when we die and enter into eternal fellowship with God in Christ in heaven; and (3) since we have been forgiven we *can* live free from sin, be happier, and accomplish definite good. None of these ideas is adequate for us. Therefore, to concentrate on these three aspects of Hebrews would be to banalize the power of the Epistle. Rather, its strength lies precisely in its preoccupation with the notions of sin and guilt and the language of myth and cult.

The notion that sin is a disturbance in the cosmic balance, which will uncannily continue to cause ripplelike, destructive effects ad infinitum unless it is redressed and the balance restored, is an early and powerful hermeneutic construction of the human imagination. It is testified to in early Hebrew cultic practices; it is ennobled in Greek tragedy; and it finds systematic statement in Anselm's classic Western theory of the atonement. It is not a notion which speaks to modern people with such self-evident vitality. We have long since been influenced by the ideas that reality is not doggedly lawful but rather is random, unpredictable, and even absurd. Beginning with the nominalists of the fifteenth century and extending through Heisenberg and Sartre, we have been given intellectual ground for this belief. Certainly the wars and catastrophes of the last six hundred years have given us ample evidence of it. The sixteenth-century Wars of Religion, the First World War, and Vietnam, all in their ways can be interpreted to show that reality is fundamentally, tragically absurd.

At the same time, most of us are not quite willing to see life as purposeless and without structure. The notions of sin and guilt, though less evident, continue to operate for us. Today they are to be found not so much in philosophy and art—and certainly not in civil religion—as in the consultation room of the psychoanalyst. Here we wrestle with issues of guilt and punishment, of sin and reparation. One of the insights won from psychoanalytic practice is that behavior motivated by guilt almost inevitably turns out to be harmful. This is not to suggest that all guilt is useless or pathological; people who do not feel guilt are lacking in the ability to experience the full range of human relations, they are psychopaths, harmful to others. It is rather that activities motivated by guilt are diffuse and have an innately unsatisfying character about them. A gift a man gives his wife because he feels guilt about having stolen from his mother years before will neither remove the guilt nor make the wife happy. The "sin" against the mother will stand yet in his memory, and his wife will unconsciously sense that the symbolic gift is somehow not an expression of feeling for her. Moreover, the husband will resent the unconscious fear which drives him to spend the money on his wife and will, probably without realizing the cause, find himself angry at her because he will perceive her as demanding, ungrateful, and insatiable.

In this vignette, psychoanalysis and mythic cult find a point of conjunction. Guilt is not only real as a feeling but is an appropriate result of certain behavior. At the same time, however, our efforts to expiate guilt tend to be self-defeating and produce more guilt. To paraphrase Paul, we need the law to let us know how to live without sinning. Yet, it is exactly through the law that we experience guilt, and our efforts to deal with our guilt cause us to sin more. Thus a vicious cycle is set up. We need some means of freeing ourselves from the past in order to deal with the future unencumbered. We need, in a word, forgiveness, a word which could suggest giving us that which is before us, namely the future.

Clearly the methods of forgiveness articulated in Hebrews and sought in psychoanalysis are different. Nevertheless, the issues are not so different. Twentieth-century people continue to struggle with sin, guilt, expiation, and forgiveness. To preach Christ is to acknowledge this, to delineate the contemporary forms of the struggle, and to offer the continuing promise of Christianity: forgiveness and a hopeful future.

Today's Gospel focuses upon a smaller section of the passion read yesterday on Palm Sunday. Unlike Hebrews, it is narrative rather than discursive. Nonetheless, its theology is carefully wrought and deals with much the same problem as the Second Lesson: how is it that Jesus, the Messiah according to the prophesies, was not recognized and was killed, and how is it that even since his coming the world remains sinful?

Taking the pericope as it stands in Mark (cf. the exegesis above for a discussion of the form-critical issues involved with vv. 3b–6), the scene opens with a reiteration of the conflict between the forces of God and the forces of Satan, which have been set against each other since Jesus' temptation in the wilderness. The chief priests and scribes, agents of the Evil One, are plotting against him. It is two days before the Passover, the feast which commemorates the victory of God in saving his people from their bondage in Egypt. At this point in the narrative the place of the people in the drama of salvation is not yet clear. What is intimated is a connection between the Exodus and the coming denouement of Jesus.

Jesus is at table with some aquaintances. Since hardly anything in Mark is entirely accidental, the fact that this Simon is a leper may be meant to remind the audience of Jesus' ministry to the diseased and outcast, especially in view of what is about to happen.

A woman enters and anoints Jesus with incredibly expensive ointment. Some at the table are indignant because her act seems a wasteful use of this stuff. It could have been sold to alleviate poverty. Jesus, in a short discourse of Marcan editorial creation, says that what the woman has done is a prophetic act; it is to signify his death.

The anointing itself must be understood as prophetic symbolism. As such, anointing is the manner of ordaining prophets, kings, and brides; Jesus is all of these. Jesus interprets this anointing as "a good work" because it condenses two significations of the symbol of anointing—ordination of Messiah and preparation for burial. The central irony of Mark's Christology and soteriology appears here: Jesus is revealed as Son of God, Savior, only in and through his utterly human death.

The other crucial element of the irony, sinful misunderstanding, is present also. Those at table with Jesus cannot recognize the truth. They are blinded by sin in a very seductive form: the urge to do good. They are put off by what they see as an improvident use of money. They wish to do good; they wish to obey not only the letter but the spirit of the law and help the poor. Thus Satan can use even the best motivation to subvert recognition of the divine. The truth of the human situation comes home again. Even our best intentions, even our most selfless efforts, even our most careful and scrupulous activities are contaminated by evil, and we are not able to recognize the presence of the divine.

Thus this Gospel articulates again the Pauline insight so true of us today: no matter what we do, it will be found to have been imperfect and sinful. Salvation will not come through trying harder or knowing more. Salvation will come, mysteriously and paradoxically, in coming to grips with our inevitable failure, our unavoidable sinfulness, and our inescapable death. It is the death, ours and Jesus', to which the woman with the ointment points and in his death our salvation is grounded.

Tuesday in Holy Week

Lutheran	Roman Catholic	Episcopal	Pres/UCC/Chr	Meth/COCU
Isa. 49:1–6	Isa. 49:1–6	Isa. 49:1–6	Isa. 42:1–9	Isa. 49:1–9a
1 Cor. 1:18–25		1 Cor. 1:18–31	1 Tim. 6:11–16	1 Cor. 1:18–31
John 12:20–36	John 13:21–33, 36–38	John 12:37–38, 42–50 or Mark 11:15–19	John 12:37–50	John 12:37–50

EXEGESIS

First Lesson: Isa. 42:1–9. For an exposition of this passage see above, pp. 17–18.

Second Lesson: 1 Tim. 6:11–16. These verses from 1 Timothy have long been regarded as an interruption of the author's thought. Amidst the discussion of riches and the love of money (v. 9–10, 17–19), the "pastor" inserts a charge to Timothy to pursue his struggle of faith to its goal, reminding him of the event at which he entered the contest and at which he had made confession. The pericope is rich in formulaic expressions, no doubt deriving from the creedal and liturgical practice of the ancient Christian community. Even when the Scriptures of the NT came to be read in the churches, brief, summarylike statements of faith or "homologies" were needed to fix what was central. The reference to God who gives life to all, the Jesus who made confession before Pilate (v. 13), is a "binitarian" formula—an anticipation of the first and second articles of the Apostles' Creed—and harks back to an ancient homology. The doxology in vv. 15–16 is suggestive of a liturgy in use in the primitive church, originally gleaned from the Hellenistic synagogue (the description of God as "blessed," having "immortality," and dwelling in "unapproachable light" appear to point in that direction). Even the "charge" to Timothy in v. 14 may not have been the author's own. Previously coined material has thus been coordinated with the author's exhortations.

Of the suggestions regarding the event in Timothy's life to which the author refers in order to spur him on, that of his appearing before a pagan tribunal seems the least, and that of his ordination the most, likely. What is at issue in these verses is not a general admonition, applicable to any situation, but one connected with a specific action in which the pupil of the apostle laid down a witness and received a commission. If the event is that of Timothy's ordination, then the similarity between the admonitions here and those appearing elsewhere in the NT suggests that the formula had its original setting in the baptismal service, the rite of ordination merely giving further shape to an obligation accruing to all Christians upon their baptism. At any rate, this event made possible the author's comparison of the passion of Christ with Timothy's conflict with the world and with false doctrine.

With his admonition to Timothy in v. 11 to "shun all this," the author creates a connection with the earlier context. The reference to Timothy as "man of God" may not intend to single him out from others, but if we allow for that "nascent Catholicism" reflected in the post-Pauline literature, the designation may reflect a concept of ordination as bestowing a special grace, and thus of Timothy as Spirit bearer or "man of God" par excellence. In contrasting what is to be shunned and what appropriated, the author in curiously un-Pauline fashion lists "righteousness" as a virtue among others at which Timothy must aim. The fact that the term appears first on the list, and thus may conceivably be interpreted as the basis for the remainder, or the possibility of its definition in terms of "proper behavior" helps nothing. For Paul, "righteousness" or "godliness" (a term the apostle never used) indicated less a possibility than a reality of Christian existence. For Paul, what was to be pursued were the "fruits" of righteousness. And as for "faith," only once does the apostle describe it in conjunction with other gifts (1 Cor. 12:9), where it may denote the capacity for working prodigies.

After reminding Timothy of his confession, the pastor appropriates the dual, binitarian formula in v. 13, in preparation for the "charge" to his addressee. The first half of the formula—"God who gives life to all things"—reflects Jewish and Christian struggle with paganism, over against which the worship of the one God had to find expression in confession. If the second half of the formula originally referred to Christ's faith and not to his behavior, then the reference to his "good confession" may have been added for the sake of the parallel with Timothy's vow. The revision thus reflected that period in the church's life when the concept of the believer's conformity to Christ was giving way to the idea of "following," or when christological statements began to be used paradigmatically.

The "commandment" indicated in the charge of v. 14 no doubt refers to Timothy's "commission of office" on the occasion of his ordination, and is thus connected with the homology of v. 12. Is Timothy being reminded of that event in the very words uttered at the time of its occurring? At any rate, the apostle's pupil is obliged to carry out his office intact ("unstained and free from reproach") till the return of Christ.

In the doxology of vv. 14–15, the formula regarding Christ's "appearing" may hark back to an older, apocalyptic tradition. Such references to Christ's return belonged to the oldest confessional statements of the early community. At first sight, however, that tense expectation of Christ's advent which characterized earliest Christianity seems dampened by the more or less indeterminate idea that God will bring it about in his own good time. The eschatological mood seems to have come loose from an imminent expectation. But if, as our author emphasizes in his introduction (1:1) and at the midpoint of his Epistle (3:16ff.), salvation proceeds from God, this hymnic formula may express less an embarrassment over the Parousia's delay than the certainty that it will indeed occur—albeit "at the proper time" (v. 15a). The author's thought finally rests in an adoration of God, rich in titularity and full of pathos, for in opposition to the deification of kings and emperors it praises the "King of kings and Lord of lords," and in resistance to sects which boast the knowledge of God it asserts that no mortal eye can bear his sight—provided he himself does not work the miracle.

Gospel: John 12:37–50. This text is comprised of two parts. The first is an epilogue to the "book of signs," which begins with the Cana miracle (chap. 2) and ends with Jesus' riding to his death earlier in this chapter. The second gives a survey, or résumé, of Jesus' public activity in the shape of a discourse. In its interpretation of Isa. 53:1 and 6:10, the first part bears striking resemblance to synoptic tradition, in which misunderstanding or unbelief is traced to prophetic prediction (cf. Mark 4:12; Matt. 13:15; Luke 8:9–10, and with specific reference to Jewish unbelief, Acts 28:26–27). The second part, or résumé, is highly reminiscent of Moses' farewell in Deuteronomy and echoes synoptic passages such as Matt. 7:26; 10:40, and Luke 10:16.

After setting the scene in v. 36, the epilogue first states the result of Jesus' activity among his own—"they did not believe in him" (v. 37). The author then marks down this result to the fulfillment of prophecy—"that the word spoken by the prophet Isaiah might be fulfilled: 'Lord, who has believed our report . . . ?' " (v. 38). Next, by interpreting Isaiah 53 in light of Isaiah 6, the evangelist roots the prophet's prediction in the divine predestination—"therefore they could not believe" (v. 39; cf. Deut. 29:1–4). He then justifies his interpretation of the prophet's word as referring to Jesus' activity—"Isaiah said this because he saw his glory and spoke of him" (v. 41). Finally, the author qualifies his initial statement with the word that "many . . . believed in him" (v. 42). Since, however, the many did not confess their faith, having "loved the praise of men more than the praise of God" (v. 43), the qualification is only apparent—the tragedy of unbelief among the Jews is unrelieved.

In the résumé the Gospel writer summarizes Jesus' public ministry in the form of a brief discourse, and in a fashion reminiscent of Moses' valedictory (cf. Deut. 32:45–47). The summary is composed of three clauses (vv. 44–45, 46–48, 49–50), the first of which expresses the idea that Jesus is the Revealer who makes God visible—"He who believes in me, believes not in me but in him who sent me. And he who sees me sees him who sent me" (vv. 44–45). A position with regard to Jesus is thus decisive for human destiny. In the second clause this thought is first expressed positively—to faith, the revelation spells light (v. 46). But this word only serves as foil for what follows in vv. 47–48—to unbelief, the revelation spells judgment. If the rejection of Jesus and his word incurs judgment, however, it is not Jesus but his word (cf. Deut. 31:19–26) which sits in judgment. The final clause makes clear that since God is encountered in Jesus, who does not speak on his own authority but only by commission of his Father, denial of Jesus is a denial of God (cf. Deut. 18:18–19).

Vv. 38–40 are an interpreter's "cross." They state that people disbelieved Jesus' words and deeds because the OT said they must. That cross is not lifted with the suggestion that this thought is primitive, indicating no awareness of secondary causality, or with the argument that purpose clauses in Hellenistic Greek eventually lose their original force, and that thus the evangelist is not stating a full doctrine of predestination. Nor is that cross eased with the recognition that the argument is not to be interpreted in psychological fashion, as if the reader were being prodded to take inventory, and in such fashion awakened to responsibility. For the Fourth Gospel, Jewish unbelief is not an accidental datum. The rejection of Messiah by his own people ought not to take anyone familiar with the OT by surprise. More, not content with merely describing the disbelief of Jesus' own as the fulfillment of prophecy, the evangelist anchors the prophet's foresight in the inevitability of the divine decree. There is no avoiding the difficulty: in the Fourth Gospel, the story of Jesus has its cause and its consequence in the impenetrable, ordaining will of the Father. But perhaps there is more to be said here than that the Fourth Evangelist has drawn the limit to our understanding and enjoined us only to silence or worship. "John" conceives the grace and truth which came in Jesus as present in the realities of life—in unbelief, death, and judgment—as actually pressing such realities into their service. More important, in the NT the last (chronologically, the first) word on predestination is not contained here, in the synoptists, or in Acts, but rather in Romans: Israel's unbelief is the means of Gentiles' coming to faith, an unbelief itself someday to be overcome by the very One who decreed it (Romans 9—11).

In the first servant song of Isaiah 42, the figures of the mediator of the word and mediator of the deed, once converging in the story of Moses but long separated in Israel's history, again come together in that mysterious servant, for whose portrait a host may have sat, and who the Christian community announced had appeared in Jesus, the proclaimer and embodiment of the decisive world-historical deed of God. For the fourth evangelist, the "signs" and "sayings," or spoken deeds of this Jesus—whose "glory" was seen by the author of the fourth servant song (Isa. 53:1)—uncover faith and unbelief, determine life and judgment for the world. In the Cyrus song, Second Isaiah conceives the salvation intended by God as political. As such, the song is not directly transferable to Jesus Christ. But the political is clearly not the only aspect within the prophet's horizon. Elsewhere, he writes that the "light of the nations" is given in order that Yahweh's salvation may reach "to the ends of the earth" (cf. 49:6). It is just such a picture which the Fourth Gospel applies to Jesus, who "cried out and said, '. . . I have come as light into the world, that whoever believes in me may not remain in darkness' " (12:44–46).

HOMILETICAL INTERPRETATION

Again, the prophecy of the servant-Messiah sets the ironic tone for today's Second Lesson and Gospel. The same questions are asked: Why was Jesus not recognized? And why, for all his suffering, is the world now no different from the way it has been? The first is a profound question for the Christian; the second is a wrenching question for every human being. So as yesterday we saw two attempts to deal with these questions proffered in Hebrews and Mark, today's readings choose two different approaches: 1 Timothy and John.

Seen by itself, the Timothy passage seems to court the indictment of empty exhortation. As an answer to the difficult life-and-death questions posed by Holy Week, this passage can be read as though it came from a football coach: "Try harder." To do so would be to miss reading this passage in its two natural contexts, the history of the church and its liturgical place in the paschal lections.

First Timothy comes from a time when the church's perennial problem, the delay of the Parousia, had to find an alternative to the sense of eschatological immediacy of Paul. It was, as the exegesis suggests, a time when the eschatological mood had come loose from imminent expectation. The earliest church had operated with a Jewish sense of reality and thought in terms of time and history. The Parousia and the Kingdom of God were coming in the future. The church was the body which knew that and already experienced in anticipatory terms the fruits of the age to come—love, joy, and community. As the Parousia delayed, a subtle but important shift in the church's mentality took place. Increasingly the tension between "this age" or "this world" and "the world to come" was not experienced as entirely a tension between two *times* but as a tension between two coexistent *worlds:* the secular world of pagan gods, political power, and self-serving behavior; and the sacred world of the church.

The church was contained within the world but was not of it; it was a creation of the Spirit. It was characterized by purity and separation from the secular. Its members were reborn through baptism, and this sacramental identification with Jesus Christ changed their citizenship and their very identity so that they too were no longer of the secular world, though they continued to have to live in it physically. This movement can be detected even in Luke and certainly in John. By the time of Hippolytus in the early third century, it is the dominant self-understanding of the church. The Easter baptisms are of candidates who have been chosen for their character, who have been on trial for years, and who in the days of Holy Week undergo a series of privations and exorcisms designed to sever their connection from the world. At the Vigil of Easter they are baptized nude, clothed in garments symbolic of their new identity, and sealed with oil against the spiritual powers of the secular world. The Parousia is not denied; it has become secondary to an understanding of identity in which salvation is equated with belonging to the church, manifesting a certain holy character, and withstanding the very real temptations and dangers of a persecuting secular world.

First Timothy is a document from a church which is on its way toward the third century. It is beginning to breathe a spirit of self-understanding in which enduring persecution and "witnessing a good confession," that is, confessing Christ when hauled before the authorities, were becoming the central themes of Christian identity. Salvation was becoming a sense of righteousness and vindication *based in* enduring the slanders and persecutions of a sinful world. The Christian's sense of freedom and victory came from facing death and accepting it while not hating those who were about to kill him or her. It was a powerful sense of superiority, based in suffering and grounded in a community which saw itself as modeled after the One who confessed and suffered paradigmatically: Jesus Christ. To suffer bravely and in love became, for the pre-Constantinian church, both the means of and the proof of salvation.

With Constantine, of course, things changed radically. The church was no longer persecuted but was honored and charged with the task of caring for the evil, secular world from which it had only recently seen itself as ontologically separate. The issue of Christian character, the questions of endurance and suffering became matters of personal, ascetic activity. The medieval notions of mortification and holiness were a transformation of the spirit of the sectarian church to a level of personal spiritual progress in imitation of Christ. At the same time, however, the church as caretaker of the world saw its mission as the establishment of justice, the merciful care of the sick and helpless, the correction of public vice, and so on. From then until now, Christians have been caught on the horns of the double identity. In Holy Week the tension surfaces again. We are tracing the story of the last days of a man who was misunderstood, tortured, and killed by the world. At one time, the church understood its identity to be in conforming itself to that model. Assuming the world was unalterably evil, salvation consisted in separating from the world and exposing oneself to humiliation, suffering, and even death at its hands, thereby convicting the world of sinfulness and achieving vindication oneself. At the next moment in its history, the church was to find its identity in being the soul of the world. First Timothy breathes the spirit of the pre-Constantinian sectarian church, in which suffering was of itself a mark of holiness. We live in a post-Constantinian church in which, if anything, suffering tends to be, in shades of the Deuteronomic theology, a sign of some sin or fault such as laziness, irresponsibility, or emotional illness.

The questions raised by the presence of 1 Timothy in the context of Holy Week, then, are these: What does it mean for us to "witness"? And what are we to make in our world of such long-suffering virtues as faith, love, patience, meekness? Our temptation is to exhort their value for their own sake. This would work in the church of Timothy or Hippolytus or in an eighth-century Benedictine monastery. It does not make immediate sense to a twentieth-century person who does not connect suffering with moral superiority. Each preacher will, of course, have to deal with this question in terms of his or her own theology. It is worth remembering, however, that the church has never been utterly without the word that Christ died for the world and for all people. Perhaps the dialectic of pre-Constantinian and post-Constantinian ecclesiologies suggests a synthesis. Perhaps to witness a good confession in our time is, in fact, to be willing to suffer for the betterment of the world, acknowledging full well that the world will neither thank us much nor change a bit for all our efforts. Our efforts will be Christian witness.

In turning from the Second Lesson to the Gospel, we find yet another perspective on the questions raised for us by the messianic prophecies and the apparent tragedy of Jesus' life and death. John seems to begin with a simple and ultimately unhelpful declaration that Jesus was not recognized, that he suffered and died because God had ordained that it would happen this way. Furthermore, not entirely unlike the late church of Hippolytus in Rome, this theologian of Alexandrian Christianity seems to propose that the purpose of Jesus' coming was to occasion judgment. John says that to recognize and believe in Jesus was to be saved and that not to do so was to damn oneself.

At this juncture the preacher has two hermeneutical choices. He or she can move to the right, so to speak, and talk in terms of the exclusive claim which Jesus makes as the Revealer of salvation. Here traditionally is preached the necessity for accepting Jesus Christ as Lord and Savior, since when confronted by his words, one must say either yea or nay. To hear Jesus preached is to be in an hour of decision, and only accepting him will bring freedom and joy. This is the traditional evangelical use of John, and it is consistent with a dominant theme in that Gospel's theology; salvation is an individual and largely secret or subjective matter. One cannot describe salvation objectively, nor can one even allude to it parabolically as do the synoptics. Salvation has to be experienced to be understood, and John's Gospel is about the task of pointing the way to that experience: knowing and accepting Jesus as the Christ, the Revealer of God. According to this interpretation, time and history are ephemeral. Jesus is eternal and real and ever re-presented for our decision. To accept him is to be ushered into eternal salvation; one is either saved or not.

Though this reading is at least partly faithful to the near-Gnostic spirit of John, it does not do justice to the historical context of Holy Week within which this reading is set. Holy Week is an anamnesis, a calling back into the present of a series of events which happened in a time past. As such, it is not just concerned with what happens to you or to me in this moment of time, but it has to do with what might happen to us as a result of what has happened in the past. The Fourth Gospel opens with a hymn to the incarnation. John, more thoroughly than any of the other Gospels, grounds his theology in the notion that in Jesus the divine became human. Even though his incarnate Jesus seems often uncomfortably docetic, John wants to insist that he is human, that he weeps, that he is "moved in his guts," that he loves and suffers. Thus for John salvation comes in human form.

In fact it is precisely the humanness of the form that blinds the eyes and hardens the hearts of those who do not recognize him. They have their own expectations of Messiah: power, perfect obedience to the letter of formal law, and so on. Because he acts with compassion and heals on the Sabbath, they are offended and reject him. They cannot find a possibility of salvation in suffering, or power in weakness. They wish to escape their own humanness and avoid their own deaths by identifying with a Savior who will not suffer and cannot die. They cannot see the ultimate moment of the incarnation—that God's greatest glory is revealed in that moment when his Son is pinned in utter helplessness to the instrument of his death. His lifting up in glory is ironically equated with his being lifted up on the cross. They cannot imagine that God's greatest power would be in identifying with humanity's greatest humiliation—death. In denying Jesus as the Christ, they deny their own humanity which God stands ready to affirm and bless. In this reading of John, the birth of Jesus, the incarnation as an historical event leading to the events of Holy Week, the very nature of human existence change. From the time of Jesus on, our humanity—precisely in its weakness and dying—becomes the vehicle of salvation. Here in the context of Holy Week, John and Mark, the latest and the earliest of the Gospels, find an essential point of contact: the irony of Jesus' death's being the manifestation of his saving power and identity. To find God in that tortured human figure on that hideous cross is to believe that in the depths of our own lonely humiliations and powerless dying God will be present, the God who raised up Jesus from the dead.

Wednesday in Holy Week

Lutheran	Roman Catholic	Episcopal	Pres/UCC/Chr	Meth/COCU
Isa. 50:4–9a	Isa. 50:4–9	Isa. 50:4–9a	Isa. 52:13—53:12	Isa. 50:4–9
Rom. 5:6–11		Heb. 9:11–15, 24–28	Rom. 5:6–11	Rom. 5:6–11
Matt. 26:14–25	Matt. 26:14–25	John 13:21–35 or Matt. 26:1–5, 14–25	Luke 22:1–16	John 13:21–38 or Matt. 26:1–5, 14–25

EXEGESIS

First Lesson: Isa. 52:13—53:12. This passage, by all odds the best known portion of the Book of Isaiah, comprises the fourth servant song. It contains a report concerning the servant (53:1–11a), framed by a word of God (52:13–15 and 53:11b–12) which echoes the designation of the servant in song one (42:1–4). The report and its frame are linked by the fact that the one unfolds and interprets the other. Thus, vv. 2–5 and 10–11a of the report correspond to vv. 14 and 15 of the frame. In addition, v. 15 of the frame furnishes the report in 53:1 with its introduction.

In its form, the report is reminiscent of OT thanksgiving psalms. The fact that it is uttered in the third person, however, distinguishes it from OT thanksgiving, for here it is not the one rescued who tells his story but those for whom what occurred to the sufferer spelled rescue. But this means that the context of the fourth servant song is eschatological—the servant's plight is told from the viewpoint of his exaltation or victory. Only from this eschatological point of view, from the standpoint of the end, can the significance of the song be properly grasped.

The introduction or superscription in v. 13 ("Behold, my servant shall prosper," or better, "my servant is victorious!") is followed by an announcement or proclamation in vv. 14–15. The announcement describes the event of the servant's humiliation and exaltation indirectly, that is, in terms of its effects on those who witnessed it—as great as was their surprise at his humiliation (v. 14), so great is their astonishment at his exaltation (v. 15).

The actual report or confession begins with 53:1, which marks the strangeness of the event and concludes with v. 11a ("he shall see the fruit of the travail of his soul and be satisfied"). V. 2, in a fashion characteristic of the ancient patriarchal narrative, states the preconditions for the servant's subsequent fate in a physiological note—"he grew up . . . like a young plant, and like a root out of dry ground; he had no form or comeliness . . . no beauty . . ." To this meanness in form corresponds the confessors' reaction to the servant in v. 3: "He was despised, and we esteemed him not." In vv. 4–6, the alternation of pronouns ("he," "we") gives a clue to the witnesses' discovery that nothing less than the atoning power of God was manifest in this man whose suffering brought him such revulsion. How the circle of witnesses came to their discovery is as much a mystery as the servant's real identity. The most that can be said is that the confessors' recognition that they were in the wrong while the despised sufferer bore their guilt and thus created their peace must have dawned on them at the moment of his exaltation. Vv. 7–8 introduce a new note—the servant's suffering consisted not merely in sickness or disease, in being "smitten by God," but as with the psalms of lament, in being hounded and opposed by his enemies. In vv. 8–10 the servant's death is described as that which corresponds to his beginning—just as was his suffering, so his death was that of an innocent man. Finally, vv. 10b–11 announce the servant's exaltation following his death—an event for which nothing furnished preparation, to which nothing in the servant's career of suffering gave the slightest clue, an event whose origin and explanation lay only in God: "It was the will of the Lord to bruise him," and "the will of the Lord shall prosper in his hand." Yahweh himself is the only bridge which leads from the servant's suffering and death to his new life.

The song concludes with the word of Yahweh in v. 11b (perhaps best translated, "my servant will show himself to be righteous . . . and so stand as righteous before the many") and in v. 12. This conclusion radically de-sacralizes the notion of sacrifice and overturns the temple cultus. The offering for atonement does not consist in animals or vegetables which man offers to God in the cult of the temple but it consists in the scorned existence of a man disfigured by suffering. He is an atonement offering: "He bore the sin of many, and made intercession for the transgressors."

The influence of this text upon the Christian community can scarcely be overemphasized. It is reflected in the Lord's Supper tradition (cf. Mark 14 and pars), in that tradition which viewed the healing of the sick against the background of the servant's suffering (cf. Matt. 8:16–17), in the *imitatio* tradition (cf. 1 Peter 2), and in the christological tradition itself. The first narrators of the passion omit any express reference to Isaiah 53, but their dependence on the fourth song is so patent that it can be said that this prophecy gripped the primitive Christian community with an original force precisely where it was not directly cited. The conscious identification of Christ with the servant of Isaiah was inevitable. For if the servant was exalted as lord ("my servant is victorious," 52:13; "I will divide him a portion with the great," 53:12), that lordship was inextricably bound up with his "substitution" ("he has borne our griefs and carried our sorrows"). Substitution was the central presupposition of his lordship, and his lordship the goal of his substitution: "Being found in human form he humbled himself and became obedient unto death. . . . Therefore God has highly exalted him and bestowed on him the name which is above every name" (Phil. 2:8–9). In his exposition of the song, Luther put it squarely: "This passage summarizes the entire gospel. . . . Since then nothing else has been said and treated of than this sentence: 'My Servant, the righteous one. . . .'"

Second Lesson: Heb. 9:11–15, 24–28. In Hebrews 9:24–28 (for the comments on vv. 11–15, see above on pp. 18–20) the implicit connection between Jesus as "pioneer" and Jesus as "perfecter" (12:1–6) or "high priest" (9:11–15) becomes explicit. He is described on the one hand as having appeared "to put away sin by the sacrifice of himself" (v. 26), and on the other as about to appear to save those who are "eagerly waiting for him" (v. 28). These concepts seem merely to occur in tandem, but in reality they are intimately related. It is precisely because the community has been purified by Christ's high-priestly activity that it is enabled to run the "race" set before it, or that it eagerly awaits his second appearing. Only when the motif of the community's journey toward its heavenly goal is linked in such fashion with Christ's high priesthood can the apparent tension between the two concepts be resolved.

If, as has been eloquently argued, the eschatological motif provides the basis for the portrait of Christ as High Priest, it is nevertheless that portrait which gives to the eschatological motif its dialectical character, since by virtue of Christ's death, believers not merely hasten toward but are already in possession of their goal: "But you have come to Mount Zion and to the city of the living God, the heavenly Jerusalem" (12:22). For this reason, Christ is no longer only Pioneer but also Lord of the community which he has freed from sin, and which thus may follow him (see above on pp. 8–10 the remarks about 12:1–6).

Earlier, biblical scholars assumed that the originality of the author of Hebrews lay in his application of the title of priest to Christ. But the fact that the Epistle introduces the title so abruptly, without introduction (cf. 2:17), militates against such an opinion—the transference of the title is presupposed as already known. In addition, there is ample evidence that the concepts of Messiah or Christ and high priest were already joined before our author put pen to paper. And as for the liturgy of the community which furnished the vehicle for his interpretation, it merely reflected a link already forged in the literature of Judaism.

In the description of Christ's high priesthood in these verses, two apparently contradictory notions appear. The first concerns his function in the heavenly sanctuary: "Christ has entered . . . into heaven itself, now to appear in the presence of God on our behalf" (v. 24): and the second refers to his crucifixion: "He has appeared . . . to put away sin . . . having been offered once to bear the sins of many" (vv. 26 and 28). The contradiction is resolved in the author's view of Jesus' death as the beginning of his exaltation or ascension. For if, as 9:11–15 makes clear, Christ's death is both the "hindrance" to the heavenly world *and* the entry into that world, then his self-sacrifice is already a component of the heavenly high priesthood.

The originality of the author of Hebrews does not consist so much in his invention of new ideas as in his pressing into the service of the gospel ideas and concepts alien to it, and thus urging the gospel's superiority over its ancient contexts, whether of law or myth. So here Jesus' sacrifice of himself and his intercession within a sanctuary not made with hands are mutually embracing themes. Accent upon the self-sacrifice preserves the heavenly priesthood from dissolving into myth, and accent upon the high-priestly office gives to the self-sacrifice its transcendent force. Once again, law and myth have broken upon the death of Jesus of Nazareth, but whereas the myth took its origin from the fear of death, the law which recognized the presence of sin as hindrance to life with God proved the better vehicle for the message of Hebrews.

Gospel: John 13:21–38. This text falls logically into three parts. Vv. 21–30 contain a prophecy of Jesus' betrayal, vv. 31–35 a brief "farewell discourse," and vv. 36–38 a prediction of Peter's denial.

In the first part, the fourth evangelist gives shape to the idea that discipleship does not guarantee immunity in a scene at which Jesus prophesies: "Truly, truly, I say to you, one of you will betray me." None dares ask the betrayer's identity, until Peter makes secret inquiry through the disciple "whom Jesus loved." Underlying the description is the author's commitment to Peter's primacy—the disciple "whom Jesus loved" does not venture to penetrate the mystery until summoned by Peter, and at the conclusion of the Gospel he merely stoops to look into the tomb until Peter enters it (20:5–6). It is here that we first encounter that figure of the "beloved disciple" (cf. 19:26; 20:2, and 21:24; with this figure the "other disciple" in 18:15–16 and the witness by the cross in 19:35 are probably not to be identified, since they do not receive the further appellation "whom Jesus loved"). Attempts at identification of this disciple have resulted in failure, which means simply that the evangelist's intent that he remain anonymous has been preserved. It does not mean, however, that the anonymous disciple is merely an ideal figure. He is ideal to the degree that he furnishes a foil to Peter and an example to the reader, but for the portrait of that one who always sees when others are blind, and always believes when others doubt, someone of real flesh and blood has sat. The subsequent narrative in vv. 26–30 is concerned less with Judas's person than with his act, which is then described in a twofold way: first, in the statement that after the morsel Satan entered into him; then in Jesus' summons, "What you are going to do, do quickly."

If the Gospel of John is tell-like in character, if more than one hand is responsible for its composition, then vv. 28–30 may be the author's own insertion into his source, since the beloved disciple's knowledge of Judas as betrayer (an obvious inference from v. 26) and his subsequent ignorance reported in v. 28 do not agree. Or are we to construe this disciple's inactivity following the revelation of the betrayal as derived from his recognition of its involuntary character? At any rate, Judas's deed is removed from the sphere of the human or psychologically motivated—with the taking of the morsel, Satan is the subject of the action, and his entry into Judas is the counterpart to the disciple's "abiding." What Judas does following Jesus' summons is not reported. He will appear again only in 18:2 and 5. The section closes with words which may have been in the tradition but which had profounder meaning for the evangelist than for his source: "And it was night"—the night which put an end to Jesus' earthly work.

In the second part of the text, the evangelist tersely describes Jesus' departure, the attendant distress of the disciples, and the way to its conquest in the command to love. The appearance of the temporal adverb "now," and the alternation in tenses of the verb "glorify" in vv.

31 and 32, impede understanding until it is seen that in the one verse the evangelist collapses the imminent and distant future (Jesus' death, resurrection, and Parousia) into the present—"now is the Son of man glorified"—and in the other returns to events in the last night of Jesus' life—"God will also glorify him." Here again (cf., for example, 17:1) the evangelist invests the term "glory" with that paradoxical quality characteristic of his Gospel, and according to which it spells the cross of the Son by whose obedience God receives his due, with the result that both Father and Son are glorified. In this fashion, perhaps, the author corrects the more "naive" view of Christian eschatology, which awaited the revelation of Jesus' glory only from the Parousia.

For the disciples, however, the "now" is still unclear; the interval between Jesus' "departure" and his final appearing persists. The crucifixion will reduce their expectations to the level of Judaism which still awaits the Christ ("as I said to the Jews so now I say to you, 'Where I am going you cannot come' "). To the question, how can the disciples' relation to Jesus be sustained in midst of this distress? vv. 34–35 give the answer: "A new commandment I give to you." This commandment is new not by virtue of its having lately appeared on the scene but by virtue of the One who gives it. "Newness" is used qualitatively (note the description of the commandment as "new" and yet "old" in 1 John 2:7–8). But if the commandment is not a recently discovered principle or cultural ideal, if it is not even new within the context of sacred history, it is not on that account "old" or without effect on the historical process. Precisely because Jesus reveals the qualitatively new on the occasion of his passion and death, the historical occasion itself takes on the character of the totally new. For the evangelist, "newness" is not unhistorical but rather eschatological in character. It implies a dynamic or energy which penetrates history and propels it toward its goal. Again, the new commandment is an eschatological commandment, because the One who gives it is about to be sacrificed in order to create that order or arrangement by which God establishes his relationship to the world in an ultimate or final way. And by virtue of their relation to Jesus, the disciples belong to that new creation and thus to each other.

The final portion of the text dramatizes the concept of discipleship. Peter's questions in vv. 36 and 37, though they reckon with the possibility of death as a consequence of adherence to Jesus ("I will lay down my life for you"), reflect a misconception of the nature of discipleship itself. The disciple assumes that following Jesus has merely to do with one's own resolution ("why cannot I follow you now?")—to which Jesus replies that he must wait ("you shall follow afterward"). More important, Peter misunderstands the "where" or goal of Jesus' departure, which collapses the future into the present. For only when the Revealer has gone to his glory, imminent *and* future, can the disciple follow him. Because of this misunderstanding of discipleship, Peter construes his "following" in terms of a heroic deed—to which Jesus finally responds that Peter will deny him three times. The beauty of the scene lies in the fact that the revelation of Peter's denial does not alter his fellowship with Jesus. The other disciples will retain fellowship with Peter after his fall precisely because Jesus had already done so at the prophecy of his fall. To accent that truth, the Gospel writer sets the prediction of Peter's denial ahead of the discourses which follow.

In the OT there are divergent views regarding judgment and salvation. According to one view, one or more righteous persons can avert the judgment due the unrighteous (Gen. 18:20–33 and Jer. 5:1), and according to another, only the righteous will be saved (Ezek. 14:12ff. and Zeph. 2:3). In Isaiah's fourth servant song the two strains are wedded: the righteous one averts what is due the unrighteous by himself suffering the punishment of God. But if Isaiah sings of a servant who had already met death when the song was composed—the author himself, Deutero-Isaiah, Israel?—the Christian community and thus the writer of Hebrews assigns the activity of bearing "the sins of many" (Heb. 9:28) to Jesus of Nazareth.

Further, if it is Yahweh or his will alone which explains the transition from the servant's humiliation to his exaltation (hence the astonishment of the "confessors" in Isa. 53:1: "Who has believed what we have heard?"), for the fourth evangelist Jesus' glorification consists in his obedience to the Father's will, thus in his death, by which God receives the glory due to him. Thus for "John" as well, Yahweh remains the sole link between the death and victory of the "Son of man"—that human destiny should be penetrated in a saving way by this death was a matter for revelation.

Finally, if in the Isaiah song the humiliation and exaltation of the servant are conceived as two separate or discrete events, for the Epistle writer and the evangelist they have become one: in Hebrews, the death of Jesus signals the commencement of his exaltation, and in the Fourth Gospel the "glorification" of the Son embraces his death as well as his resurrection and final return.

HOMILETICAL INTERPRETATION

Wednesday in Holy Week marks the turning point in the week. Since the liturgy of Palm Sunday set in motion the dramaturgical reenactment of the passion, we have paused for reflection and preparation. Tomorrow, the representation of the Last Supper will inaugurate the uninterrupted sequence of Jesus' death: supper, betrayal, vigil in Gethsemane, arrest, ordeal with Sanhedrin and Pilate, humiliation, crucifixion, death, and burial. These will come without pause as if in a symphony's finale in which crescendo and increased tempo collaborate to bring to final recapitulation and culmination all the themes that have appeared in various forms and relationships to this point. Today's readings begin this heightened intensity. The First Lesson is Isaiah's fourth servant song, the most tantalizingly "Christian" of any passage in the prophetic corpus. The Second Lesson continues Hebrew's theologizing upon the sacrificial nature of Jesus' death with the implications for us which appeared in our readings on Sunday and Monday. The Gospel marks John's last appearance this week and actually begins the events of the passion in that it narrates a portion of the Last Supper, including Judas's betrayal and the prediction of Peter's denial.

In and of itself, and highlighted by its setting in the Holy Week liturgy, the fourth servant song condenses a universal human question and a particularly Christian one. The universal question concerns suffering in all its permutations and combinations. From the beginning of the human odyssey we have asked why there is suffering. Answers have ranged from the suggestion that suffering is not real, that it is in some sense illusory or that it is inexplicable and must be met with some form of resignation, to suggestions that it is the result of or proof of misconduct, that it is the result of a malevolent force (Satan, evil, and so on), or that it is the result of an incompleteness or flaw in creation. It belongs to the genius of Hebrew theology to suggest that in some form or other human suffering could be redemptive, that is, purposeful. As every reader of Deuteronomy and Job knows, Hebrew thought tended to see suffering as proof of and punishment for some sin or disobedience. Whatever its disadvantages, this theology had a certain purchase on reality which was important—human actions do matter. The power of the Deuteronomic ethic was its sense that what we do to our environment, to one another, and to ourselves does have repercussions. Any psychoanalyst, environmentalist, or historian will agree in some sense with the dictum "The sins of the parents are visited upon their children." Any move either to deny the reality of suffering or to provide a strategem for resigning ourselves to it, as Eastern religions have tended to do, runs against the grain of our Western personality. We sense that suffering is real: children with leukemia, families in want because of war or famine, or old people burned in hotel fires are all real and tragic. We Westerners are not able to say either that such things are illusory or that they simply "must" happen. We are not able to resign ourselves to them. Our social-service structures, our medical sciences, and our vast educational establishment are proof of this.

Nevertheless, the Deuteronomic ethic had a terrible flaw; it assumed a simple one-to-one relationship between sin and suffering. Each suffering was a sign of a sin committed by the sufferer or parents or clan members. The sufferer was then understood as guilty and suffered double. Job is the paradigm; his friends might have been well-intentioned and even sympathetic, yet they could only advise him to confess his fault. In the end he was isolated. In Jesus' time, lepers were the paradigms of suffering sinners. They were ostracized from their community for fear that their sin and punishment would contaminate others. It was assumed that if they got well, it was because they had repented and God had forgiven them. In our day this Deuteronomic understanding still subtly operates. Those who suffer, the old, the mentally ill, the incompetent are institutionally isolated so as not to contaminate us. In more demonic form, we say that the poor and disadvantaged suffer a plight of their own making and excuse ourselves from responsibility to do more than take palliative or charitable measures. In effect, we Deuteronomize by thinking they are getting what they deserve.

The author of the fourth servant song accepted the Hebrew understanding that suffering is real and in some sense is involved in a chain of cause and effect. The revolutionary thing about the suffering servant is a paradoxical reversal of the cause-effect sequence. Instead of his suffering being the effect of sin, it becomes the cause of forgiveness. The servant, being righteous, suffers the punishment for those who are sinful, thereby saving them from the necessity of enduring their own deserved punishment. In one stroke the way is opened for two new ideas: (1) at least some human suffering is not brought on by the sufferer, and (2) such suffering is potentially redemptive. In this light the Christians were able to begin to comprehend the place of the cross in the economy of salvation. So too the early Christians were able to give meaning and purpose to their own suffering. So too was someone as contemporary as Martin Luther King, Jr., able to provide a vision whereby the sufferings of Blacks could be seen as the means of interrupting the malignant and sinful chain of racial cause and effect in America and provide a means whereby we could be free from the guilt of our past and enabled to make of our society a beloved community. The notion that there is the possibility of redemption in suffering strikes a profound and universal chord in each of us.

The uniquely Christian question to which the fourth servant song seemed to provide some answer was the question of why the Christ was unrecognized, misunderstood, and killed. The suffering servant was a *prediction* of the Christ, and indeed, all that Christ underwent was in conformity to that prophecy and was necessary in order for the redemptive work of suffering to take place and for him to be provided the opportunity for his eventual victory in the resurrection.

On this eve of the finale of the passion, the preacher would do well to consider the issue which will stand before us for three grim days: why did this Jesus have to suffer and die? The notion of redemptive suffering and sacrificial death is one purchase on this mystery. Its classical locus is here in the middle of Holy Week and in the fourth servant song.

The author of the Hebrews passage addresses this theme and offers one answer couched in cultic and mythological terms. Jesus' suffering and dying was the ultimate and final act of redemptive suffering; none other is necessary. The author is able to make this statement because he sees Jesus' death in the perspective of the Parousia. Christians live "between the times"; their former sins and their consequent involvement in the vicious cycle of sin and suffering have been interrupted once and for all by the sacrificial suffering of Jesus the Christ. They are now empowered to live good and brave lives in the expectation of his return to rule a world finally free from sin, death, and suffering.

Here the difficulty for the modern preacher is essentially the same difficulty the church has always experienced with the delay of the Parousia. No matter what we profess doctrinally, it is a subjective fact that we can no longer bring ourselves to expect Jesus to return at any moment. In fact, for many of our hearers, the substitute notion of persevering bravely through this life in order to gain entrance to heaven has lost much of its power. Rather, we are thrown back upon the original mystery: the universality of deathly human suffering and our innate, internal protest against it. With this the image of the crucified and dying Jesus continues to resonate. To know he suffered and died is to validate our own experience. To confess that the one who so went to humiliation is Lord and High Priest is to confess a deep, moving hope: our suffering and death are not meaningless.

In turning to the John passage we move as before from discursive to narrative theology. With this reading we begin the narratives of the passion per se. Unlike the synoptic accounts, "John's" version of the Last Supper does not focus on the eating of the meal itself, but on the foot washing and the connected "new commandment" to love one another. The emphasis in John, then, is not potentially sacramental as much as it is ethical. This is to say that the constituting force of the church as it is foreshadowed in John's Last Supper narrative is the behavior of Christ's "own" toward one another rather than their participation in the eucharistic meal. The Johannine linkage is fairly clear: one's relationship with God depends on one's response to Jesus; in the physical absence of Jesus, one's relationship to him is manifested by one's treatment of the brothers and sisters. This is the import of Jesus' postresurrection triplication to Peter of the question and command, "Do you love me? . . . Feed my sheep."

Obviously such a theology could turn into an ungraceful Pelagianism in which we struggle to love one another and find that in our continuing sinfulness we cannot and are therefore the perpetrators of our own condemnation. John seeks to avoid this danger by presenting salvation as a divinely controlled process. Thus in today's Gospel the ultimate unloving act is Judas's betrayal; Jesus foresees it, in a sense controls it himself and its cause is Satan. Likewise Peter announces his devotion to Jesus even to death, and Jesus calmly predicts his triple betrayal. All is presented with the measured pace of a process which is ordained and which is working itself out. Salvation through the death and resurrection of Jesus takes place beyond human comprehension, despite human interference, and yet, paradoxically, through human activity.

The preacher working with John in Holy Week is thus confronted with a very different spirit from what she or he will encounter tomorrow and Friday in Mark and Luke. There we will find opportunity to identify with the betrayed, suffering, and dying Jesus, to find in his death a mirror of meaning for our own. In John, on the other hand, we find an icon, a kind of semiopaque window onto a cosmic process which is working itself out beyond and beneath us. The wonder is that its ultimate goal is for our good, for our salvation. Jesus has come into our human situation; he shares our life and death. By dying our death he will make it possible for us to rise with him. It is done by God for us. Our task is only to recognize it and respond in obedience. The command which will signify our obedience and hence our status is "Love one another." In a sense, nothing *depends* on this: we will be empowered to do it. Peter could not love Jesus to the death, yet was empowered after the resurrection to "feed the sheep" and finally to follow exactly in Jesus' way, to a crucifixion.

In the passion of John, then, the preacher has the opportunity to speak of a great mystery: God is saving us, redeeming us, and empowering us in ways we do not and indeed cannot understand. The marks of that redemption are our ability to serve, our capability to love, and our capacity to recognize and follow Jesus in this world. In all cases, however, John wants to proclaim good news to us—the good news that God is our loving Father, whose will it is that we should not be lost, and who accomplishes this apart from our ability to respond. We are part of a redemptive, divine process which he promises to complete for our good. Our response, as we recognize this, will be love of him and of one another.

Maundy Thursday

Lutheran	Roman Catholic	Episcopal	Pres/UCC/Chr	Meth/COCU
Exod. 24:3–11	Exod. 12:1–8, 11–14	Exod. 12:1–14a	Deut. 16:1–8	Exod. 24:3–11 or Deut. 16:1–8
1 Cor. 10:16–17 (18–21)	1 Cor. 11:23–26	1 Cor. 11:23–26 (27–32)	Rev. 1:4–8	1 Cor. 10:16–21
Mark 14:12–26	John 13:1–15	John 13:1–15 or Luke 22:14–30	Matt. 26:17–30	Mark 14:12–26 or John 13:1–17, 34

EXEGESIS

First Lesson: Exod. 24:3–11. Chap. 24 of Exodus faces backward to the Sinai theophany in chap. 19 and forward to Moses' ascent of the mount, the construction of the golden calf, and the renewal of the covenant. In vv. 3–8 the scene is the foot of the mountain; and in vv. 9–11, on the mountain itself. Though this change of scene may reflect two originally distinct and independent literary traditions, vv. 3–8 once serving as a conclusion to the "Book of the Covenant" (cf. chaps. 20:22—23:33), in their present form both scenes are anchored in the narrative of the concluding of the covenant at Sinai.

The action in vv. 3–8 reflects the typical pattern of covenant ratification. First, Moses appears in the assembly and delivers the "words" and "ordinances" of Yahweh (v. 3a)—which in the present context include the Decalogue of 20:1ff. and the laws of 21:1ff. Second, the people consent to the "words," whereupon Moses writes them down (vv. 3b–4a). Third, an altar is built, twelve stones are erected in proximity to it, and at Moses' command sacrifices are offered on the altar by "young men of the people of Israel" (vv. 4b–5). The sacrifices consist of burnt offerings, that is, offerings totally burned up in token of the total homage which a vassal owes his lord, as well as of peace offerings, in part eaten by the cult companions, by which eating their union with God (represented by the altar) and one another is established (cf. v. 11). Fourth, the covenant is sealed in blood, of which half is sprinkled on the altar and half on the people following their assent to a new reading of the Book of the Covenant (vv. 6–8). This dividing of the blood appears to signify the covenant as an atonement as well as a binding by blood oath. At any rate, the report in vv. 6–8 is solemn, monosyllabic. Three times it is said of Moses the mediator that "[he] took. . . . and he took. . . . and [he] took"—expressions echoed in the Gospel accounts of the Last Supper (cf. Mark 14:22–23: "And as they were eating, he took bread. . . . And he took a cup. . . ."). The formula in v. 8 ("Behold the blood of the covenant . . ."), which gives the explanation to the entire action, is the same with which Jesus announces the New Covenant at his Supper (cf. Mark 14:24).

In vv. 9–11 the dual aspect of Moses' office as mediator is evident. At the altar, he had acted as God's representative. Now, together with the "chief men of the people," he ascends the mountain as representative of the community. In v. 10 the astonishing statement is made that Moses, Aaron, and the seventy elders, together with Nadab and Abihu (does the appearance of these names reflect tradition independent of the Sinai narrative?) "saw the God of Israel." The Septuagint translators weakened the expression to read, "And they saw the place where the God of Israel had stood." Others have followed suit. The passage is not without parallels, however, since the vision of Isaiah begins with the words "In the year that King Uzziah died I saw the Lord sitting upon a throne" (Isa. 6:1). But when it comes to describing what the delegation actually saw, reference is made only to what appeared "under his feet," that is, to a "pavement of sapphire stone," or transparent platform of lapis lazuli—a blue stone, clear or pure as heaven—through which one might peer from beneath. At any rate, the prepositions in v. 10 which the RSV translates "as it were" and "like" are calculated to render what was seen merely analogous to the reality. It would appear that the delegation did not dare raise its eyes to the God of Israel himself. Yet the statement in v. 10 still stands—"they *saw* the God of Israel." Further, the extraordinary character of this encounter on the mountain is hammered home in v. 11a to the effect that God did not "lay his hand on" the men on the mountain. Once again, the Septuagint translators weakened the clause to read, "not even one of Israel's chosen perished." More significant, v. 11b states that "they beheld God," which the Septuagint one last time alters to read, "they looked on the place of God."

The narrative concludes with a cryptic reference to eating and drinking, which no doubt denotes a covenant meal which Yahweh allowed Israel's delegates to hold in his presence, and by which the bond between him and Israel was fixed. The statement in v. 11b, "They beheld God, and ate and drank"—as solemn and monosyllabic as in vv. 6–8—thus signals a new avenue of fellowship with God, in contrast to the Sinai horror of chap. 19.

Second Lesson: 1 Cor. 10:16–21. The pericope properly begins with v. 14, and deals with the question of Christian participation in pagan rites. The apostle advances to the problem with an imperative construction ("shun the worship of idols," v. 14), followed by a reference to the tradition of the Lord's Supper. References to "cup" and "blood," "bread" and "body" in v. 16, as well as to "drinking the cup of the Lord" in v. 21 (the oldest designation for the Lord's Supper), are the Pauline "logarithms" for the Supper. They were not the apostle's invention but derived from what he had received, which he described in 11:23 as "from the Lord." This shorthand is reflected in all three synoptic accounts of the Supper which, though written after the Pauline Epistles, nevertheless draw on a tradition antecedent to Paul. The logarithms have their "trajectory" in the postapostolic period, for example, in the *Dialogues* of Justin (cf. *Dialogue* 41:1 and 70:4). The issue is important, since 1 Corinthians 10 is one of the few instances in the NT in which what is "from the Lord" is raised to the level of Holy Writ. For this reason, vv. 14–22 lack any reference to the OT Scripture. Finally, after this citing of the tradition, Paul heaps up strictures ("I do not want you to be partners with demons," etc., vv. 20b–21) and concludes with a reference to the God who is jealous for his honor (v. 22).

The organizing principle in this text, as well as throughout the entire chapter, is the *paradosis,* the tradition—the OT, or what is "from the Lord." This principle does more than furnish a focus or perspective for Paul's discussion of the problem. It is something he hurls into the debate in order to end the matter. He thus uses the same remedy here in chap. 10 as he had applied in chap. 4 to the Corinthians' sitting in judgment on each other ("I have applied all this to myself and Apollos for your benefit . . . that you may learn by us not to go beyond what is written," 1 Cor. 4:6). In chap. 11 Paul will hurl the *paradosis* into the confusion created by the Corinthians' refusal to distinguish their own feasts from the Supper.

In v. 14, the apostle turns from faulty Corinthian theology (according to which the Supper or baptism or both guarantee immunity from judgment in the event of moral laxity) to faulty Corinthian practice, with a "therefore"—"Therefore, seeing that the sacrament does not yield a pretext for immorality . . ." In effect, the Corinthians were on the point of corroborating the contention of Paul's opponents everywhere that the preaching of grace would lead to moral irresponsibility. Paul next applies the *paradosis* to the Corinthian habit of participating in pagan sacrifice: "The cup of blessing which we bless, is it not a participation in the blood of Christ . . . ?" (v. 16). What occurs in the Supper, Paul argues, is that participation in Christ's body and blood makes us one with him (vv. 16–17). To illustrate this truth he first draws an analogy from Jewish ritual practice. When the Hebrews (in the Greek: "Israel according to the flesh") eat the sacrifices, they share in the altar. Similarly, when the pagans make sacrifice, though that sacrifice in itself is nothing, and the god to whom they sacrifice is a nothing (v. 19), behind that sacrifice there nevertheless lurk the demons which make that nothing into something (v. 20). For this reason, participation in Christ renders participation in the demons an impossibility (the argument in 1 Cor. 6:16 respecting sexual intercourse with prostitutes is analogous). Christ will have no rival—not even in those powers which have been demythed. Any other posture, Paul concludes, renders God jealous for his honor (v. 22).

The implication to be drawn is that formal knowledge, intellectual appreciation, does not unmask a danger. To the Corinthians Paul had written, "I give thanks to God . . . that in every way you were enriched . . . with all speech and all knowledge" (1 Cor. 1:4–5). And when he concluded the Epistle, his readers would recognize whether or not he had written those words in irony. Paul agreed that possession of powers of cognition was nothing to be ashamed of. He agreed that pagan rites in themselves meant nothing at all, that the gods to whom sacrifices were paid were nonexistent, but he did believe that in the act of participation dark powers were evoked which the nonexistent was calculated to serve. For the apostle, then, knowledge was one thing, and use another. Adolf Schlatter was quite wrong when he maintained that the Reformer had translated Rom. 1:17 to read, "the righteousness of God is *taught* in the gospel," but the heirs of the Reformer are not thereby absolved of reasoning syllogistically with Aristotle in matters of faith. Once faith is clearly defined, reason is free to do its proper work. But that definition must first occur, for wherever reason is, the demons are not far behind.

Gospel: Mark 14:12–26. Relentlessly, Mark drove home his picture of the misunderstanding of the disciples and in so doing he held up a mirror to the face of his church—and ours. This picture is all the more stark and stunning because it is not relieved by a "happy ending." There is no reunion scene at the end showing Jesus with his disciples on Easter.

In preparation for his last entry into Jerusalem, Jesus sent two disciples ahead with special instructions (cf. the parallel to his first entry, Mark 11:1–10). The two disciples find everything as foretold by Jesus, which highlights his sovereignty. While his first entry into Jerusalem culminated in the announcement of the temple's destruction, his last entry will culminate in his own destruction. He knows it, but the disciples fail to comprehend it. His disciples had intended to celebrate a Passover, which is a joyful meal that recalls God's victory over God's enemies and the deliverance of his people Israel. Yet what Jesus in fact celebrates has as little to do with the Passover as Peter's confession of Jesus as the Christ has to do with Jesus' own understanding of the meaning of messiahship (cf. Mark 8:27–34). The last meal (14:17–21) focuses not on the Passover lamb, nor on the bitter herbs, nor on God's victory in the Exodus, but on the betrayer of Jesus and on the death of Jesus. Moreover, all disciples are under suspicion and ask, "Is it I?" Instead of speculating about psychological motives which prompted Judas to turn into a traitor, Mark reminds his church that betrayal is a possibility of discipleship now. Mark placed the story which cast suspicion on all disciples "while they were eating," between the preparation and the institution of the Lord's Supper. One cannot eat with Jesus without facing the possibility of betrayal. The question "Is it I?" flanked as it is by two pronouncements of Jesus concerning betrayal, is the center of this scene, its focus.

"The Son of man goes as it is written" (14:21). This locates the death of Jesus within the divine necessity. In the next sentence, his death is located in the historically contingent action of Judas's betrayal. Two perspectives are thus held in juxtaposition.

From one perspective, Judas's betrayal is an unmitigated evil and the responsibility of "that man." From another perspective, God fulfills his will, "as it is written," through this very action—and the Son of man goes to his death in conformity with God's will. These two perspectives may not be merged or played off against each other. This means that before God I cannot blame God or the devil for my evil actions. Yet faith affirms that God will triumph in spite of and even through the evil perpetrated by man.

The new beginning in v. 22 indicates that the words of the Supper were originally transmitted independently. Mark's account of the Supper is later than Paul's (1 Cor. 11:23–25) or than Luke's special source (Luke 22:15–18, 25–30), and does not have the Passover but another Jewish sacrificial meal as its model (cf. 1 Cor. 10:18). In surprising fashion, Jesus attaches to the framework of this meal these utterances on the bread and wine: "This is my body . . . . this is my blood . . ." That "is" on which Luther at Marburg laid such stress was most probably missing in the Aramaic, but what is said appears elsewhere in gospel tradition (cf. John 6:32, 48, 51). As with all of Jesus' words, we have no "protocol" here, so that our attention is directed less to form than to content—Jesus is the bread of those who are his own, and appears for them with the sacrifice of his life. The words concerning the bread and wine are thus more than a parable (that is, "my person is for you what eating and drinking are for ordinary people"), and Jesus did more than utter a blessing over the meal. He added words which interpreted the broken bread and poured-out wine as his atoning death for the many (an echo of Isa. 53:6, 11, 12). When he gave that bread and wine to the disciples, he made them participants in the atoning power of his death.

In v. 24 Jesus describes his blood as "of the covenant." The adjective "new" could legitimately be introduced here, though the term appears only in Luke (22:20). What distinguishes this covenant as "new" is the fact that it stands on an entirely different plane of the divine economy. The cultus and institutions of the old covenant were provisional and pointed to a time when God would reveal his redemptive will more completely. On the other hand, the new covenant possesses continuity with the old, since both covenants have their origin in the same divine will. Further, a dynamic aspect inheres in this new covenant, for the divine activity is now about to propel history and humankind toward their God-intended goal. Finally, this covenant which Jesus now establishes with his disciples is the last and final "arrangement" (for this definition of "covenant" see, on pp. 18–20 above, the remarks concerning Heb. 9:11–15) between God and his community. By establishing the new covenant, Jesus thus declares that the heavenly blessings which Israel believed God would pour out at the end of days are now mediated to his community through his death.

The inference to be drawn from v. 25 is that Jesus did not participate in the eating and drinking. Might his refusal to drink have reflected a "massive" hope in the imminent arrival of the end time? Did Jesus await the revelation of God for judgment and grace the more clearly his own end came into view? If so, what the "earthly" or pre-Easter Jesus may have awaited immediately prior to (or apart from) his death, the Christian community combined with his ultimate fate—it was at the cross that the exaltation of the Son of man occurred. The phrase "until that day when I drink it new" must be taken to mean more than a figurative description of the joys of the consummation. Jesus promises his disciples that in the end time they will, under totally different conditions than now exist, drink wine together in a new way.

"And when they had sung a hymn . . ." Curiously enough, in rabbinical literature the word here translated "hymn" is the same used to refer to the Great Hallel, sung following the Passover Haggada and at the conclusion of the Passover meal (that is, Psalms 114—18). The term may thus be a transliteration, not a translation. But if so, Mark's account of the Supper has a dual model. If Jesus and the disciples recited the Hallel, then those psalms which praised the God who redeemed Israel from the might of the Egyptians, the God before whose face the earth trembles, the God who saves life from death, and the God whom the heathen are called to praise—those psalms were on his lips as he departed for Gethsemane.

That avenue of fellowship omened in the text of Exodus 24 has now been realized in a "new covenant." The ambiguity which moved the Septuagint translators to attenuate the force of the ancient text—"they saw the God of Israel . . . there was under his feet as it were a pavement''—has now been removed at the Supper of the Son of man, for here the God of Israel has not merely refrained from laying ''his hand on the chief men of the people''; he has given them his own life to share—but for all that, a gift by which all other allegiances are displaced: ''You cannot drink the cup of the Lord and the cup of demons''!

HOMILETICAL INTERPRETATION

Today's liturgy begins the unbroken sequence of events which culminates in Jesus' death. On this day, traditionally at an evening service, Jesus' Last Supper with his disciples is recalled. From that Supper he goes directly to the garden of Gethsemane where he waits, alone, for his arrest. From that moment on, the action of the passion moves with almost bewildering speed: the Sanhedrin, Pilate, the crowd, the Roman soldiers, the via dolorosa, the final agony, and the death.

In the English tradition Thursday in Holy Week is called Maundy Thursday, from an old English word meaning ''commandment.'' This relates to Jesus' word ''Do this in remembrance of me'' from 1 Corinthians 11. The thematic emphasis of year B is less on commandment, that is, on the *institution* of the sacrament of Holy Communion, than on two strains of meaning of which the Eucharist forms both symbol and part. These two themes are covenant community and sacrifice. As themes in which the Eucharist participates they have the power to illuminate the relationship of Jesus' death and resurrection to our lives and to give substance to the notion of church in that relationship. As a symbol, the Eucharist has the potential to help those relationships coalesce in the lives of Christians. For this reason, preaching on these lections behooves us to tie together the themes of the readings with the liturgical action which is their context—the celebration of the Eucharist. The overarching hermeneutical principle will be the notion of covenant relationship to God; what was established for the Hebrew people in and through the saving events of the Exodus and the making of the Old Covenant through Moses is a type, or paradigm, by which to understand the incomprehensible wonder of what has been established for us in Jesus Christ.

As so often has happened in this week's lections, the First Lesson sets the stage for both Second Lesson and Gospel. Here emerge clearly the two dominant themes of the day: covenant community and sacrifice.

God has already saved this people—called them out of their slavery and delivered them from their captors. They have obeyed, but without understanding the meaning of events which are constituting them as God's own people. In other words, though God has saved them, they do not yet own the *identity* of saved people. For this to happen, a covenant must be established with their Savior. In the context of this covenant they will find community established, and within that community each person will have an identity. The main purpose of the law is not to teach wise or even exalted principles of human behavior. Rather it is to establish the behavioral threads out of which will be woven the community of Israel. These will be the people who act in a certain way because God brought them out from slavery in Egypt and gave them a promise of land that would be theirs and bound them to himself by delivering to them a series of commandments. Thus Moses is called to the mountain where he receives the commandments. These will be the substance of the covenant, the material of the community. After receiving the commandments, Moses returns to the people and recites the commandments. In effect, he offers them the "terms" of the covenant. They can say yes or no, but they cannot bargain or modify. The people give unanimous assent and promise to do all the words which the Lord Yahweh spoke to them through Moses. At this point, the formal covenant can be made.

The ritual of the covenant involves sacrifice from the very beginning. An altar is made which will symbolize the place where Israel and God will be joined. Twelve different tribes (the twelve pillars) will be joined at one altar, and they will be one people in covenant with one God. On this altar were offered two kinds of sacrifice. Burnt offerings were totally consumed by fire to fulfill one sense of the word "sacrifice"—giving up something valuable to God as a sign of utter obedience to him. Peace offerings were shared, a part burned as God's portion and another part eaten by the cultic participants. Thus the altar signified two aspects of the covenant. The people belonged to God as a vassal to a lord, and at the same time there was a sharing in the covenant. The people shared with each other and with God. The binding together in the covenant was a binding of mutuality; as the people of Israel were commanded to care for and share with each other, so God cared for them and shared with them their lives. Thus under this covenant God would be pictured through the vicissitudes of Israel's history as being in turn angry, hurt, frustrated, compassionate, and loving toward his people. Finally, in the fullness of time, God made the ultimate effort in sharing the plight of his people: he was incarnate, suffered, and died with and for us. What is implicit in the notion of the peace offering, in which human beings share the sacrificed animal with God, is made explicit in Christmas, Holy Week, and Easter.

After the sacrificial animals had been killed, Moses, now acting as priest, divided the blood in two parts. The first part he sprinkled on the altar—God's portion. He then read to the people the words to which they had agreed, and again they assented. With that, Moses sprinkled them with the other half of the blood. Now the notion of the word of commandment and the notion of the cultic, sacramental binding together of blood kin are made. The Hebrew is a Hebrew both because he or she is born of Hebrew blood and into a Hebrew history and because he or she learns, knows, and obeys the commandments. Neither will suffice without the other; God is a God of both being and doing.

It is also worth noting that the commandments in their principal forms are concerned with two things: how the people are to acknowledge Yahweh as their exclusive God and how they are to treat each other. These two are inextricably bound up: the law is not a series of rubrics on priestcraft but a set of commandments on how the participants in a covenant community are to treat each other. Thus the ethical becomes cultic and the cultic can never be separated from the ethical. When Moses reads the commandments and sprinkles the blood as two parts of one activity, he ties together forever in the Hebrew consciousness the ethical and the religious. The ground has been laid for what comes so radically with Jesus: how we treat each other is, in fact, how we are treating God.

Thus the first part of the First Lesson introduces the themes of covenant and sacrifice in such a way that Jesus' incarnation (sharing) and sacrifice (ultimate obedience to God) can be understood as that way in which we can find our identity as part of a community which is founded in his history and in our ethical and cultic response to him.

The second part (vv. 9–11) suggests yet another aspect of the eucharistic tradition. From very early on, as is witnessed by 1 Corinthians, the Lucan story of the road to Emmaus, the Didache, and other sources, the church connected the imminent return of Jesus with the community meal. As the expectation adjusted itself to more and more indefinite delay, what had been essentially a *proleptic* presence gradually became a sense of virtual presence so that by the early Middle Ages the faithful were centering their awareness of the presence of Christ in the eucharistic elements. As alien as this shift may be to Protestant consciousness, it signals a spiritual need and points to an element which was never entirely lacking in the Hebrew tradition. Though God is so holy that we could never bear his full presence, yet he *is* present and we can behold him in occasional veiled ways. Though the weight of Hebrew tradition is on the invisible, intangible presence of God in the word spoken and meant to be obeyed, still there are visual epiphanies as well. One of these occurs in our reading when Moses and seventy of the elders of Israel go up the mountain and there see, as it were, a glimpse of God through a translucent pavement. Significantly for today's liturgy, though enigmatically in its own context, this vision is connected with eating and drinking. It suggests that perhaps visions of God were associated in parts of Hebrew tradition with cultic meals. In any case, it provides for us the possibility of connecting the sense of the presence of Jesus with the eating and drinking of the Eucharist—a presence which is more than mere individual calling to mind of our images of Jesus but is, however we conceptualize it, a mode of his presence by which the church has lived for almost two thousand years.

The Second Lesson is chosen for its overtly eucharistic connection. The cup and the bread are koinonia in the blood and body of Christ. This participation in Christ makes of the Corinthians one community. The main eucharistic theme is reiterated: participation in the Eucharist is participation in the sacrifice of Christ and binds the members to him and one another in a unified community. In and of itself, this insight will "preach" but will tend to be dogmatic unless it is seen in the fullness of the Pauline context.

First Corinthians centers in one of Paul's great arguments as to the nature of the church. It is a community which alone in the world understands that it lives between the times. Now is the old age ruled by the powers of sin and death and characterized by the law passing away. The new age, already inaugurated by Jesus' resurrection, is about to dawn. It will be ruled by God through Christ and will be characterized by love, harmony, and unity. The church not only has the "knowledge" of the resurrection and therefore of the imminence of the Parousia, but the church also has the "down payment" on the coming age. That down payment is the spirit of Christ, manifested as love for one another within the community. Thus the character of the church, the spirit of love, is also the church's witness to its faith that Jesus is about to come and establish the new age. Participation in the Eucharist is both cause and effect of this identity as citizen of the coming age. Thus the culmination of Paul's long argument about the Eucharist in chap. 11 is that those Corinthians who do not lovingly care and share with one another at the meal, and otherwise, are denying their own identity as members of the new age and are defiling the witness of the church to the reality of its appearing.

Here the themes of the Old Covenant appear in a new register. Our identity is tied to a mode of relating to one another. For our Hebrew forebears this mode of relating was the law and its ethics. For us it is love one for another. As the law was founded in the initiative of God to identify and save the Hebrew people from slavery, so our love is founded in the loving initiative of God coming among us in Jesus Christ to share our human fate, sacrificing all in love. As Hebrew identity was remembered and renewed in the annual celebrations of the Passover and the weekly reflections of that feast in the Sabbath rituals, so Christian identity is formed and renewed in the yearly Easter celebrations and the weekly Sunday celebrations of the resurrection. Thus the founding sacrificial meals of the Exodus accounts and the ritual meals of Jewish life correspond to the Last Supper and post-Easter community meals of the NT and the weekly eucharistic celebrations of the church respectively. Christian identity is bound up in Christian community, and the community is constituted in the loving and sharing which both flows from and is expressed through the Eucharist.

In this context, Paul's talk about idols in our Second Lesson assumes its proportion. Our identity is in the power of love and the expectation that ultimately love will win the day. Idols represent reliance on other powers. One cannot rely on powers other than love and remain integrated in the circle of love. If love is to have the final word in the history of heaven and earth, and if Christians are those who believe this, then the ultimate criterion for our actions and judgments, that in which we put our final trust, must be love. Otherwise, we fly in the face of our own identity.

The Gospel explicitly makes the connection between the Hebrew Passover meal and the Last Supper. The fact that historically this meal probably was not a Passover meal is irrelevant in this liturgical context. For Christians, this supper was to become the foundation of the New Covenant as the Exodus meals, especially the Passover supper, were the foundation of the Old Covenant. This connection is made explicit in the "words of institution," in which Jesus transforms the meaning of a Jewish meal which recalls the Exodus and the founding of the Old Covenant into a meal which founds a New Covenant. Moreover, the basis of the New Covenant is not so much what God *has* done as what God is *about* to do. Jesus says in a tradition which antedates Mark that he will drink no more wine until he drinks it in the (imminent) Kingdom of God. Christian identity is, then, firmly fixed as an eschatological identity.

In this context, the paradox of Judas the betrayer becomes coherent. This age is ruled by the powers of sin and death, and in this Mark and Paul agree. In this age, the power of this age will have its inning. Thus to be in this age is to suffer sinful betrayal and die. In a sense Judas was only the unlucky recipient of the mantle of sin which was bound to hold sway over Jesus' life. Had not Jesus been betrayed, had he not suffered and died, then his incarnational sharing of our lot would have been at best incomplete and at worst a mockery of our plight. Thus the Son of man had to go "as it is written of him," that is, as it must with each and every one of us who lives in this age.

At the same time, it is the awful character of this age that inevitability does not excuse. The mocking irony of Satan is that he too knows the law. As Paul says, the wages of sin is death. Thus Judas will not be protected because he acts under the sway of sin; rather, woe to him! It may be unfair, but it is the way things are, under the law, in this age. Thus the eschatological dimension of the Christian gospel becomes even more radical. It requires nothing less than a transformation of this age into the age to come for the power of sin and death to be undone. The spirit of love comes out of the future and is impractical in this age. Nevertheless, it is the spirit by which God raises from the dead, and it is the spirit which constitutes the new community and identifies those who belong in it. Thus the Eucharist, which is the pivot of this day's liturgical action, is rightly identified in the tradition as "the sacrament of love."

Good Friday

Lutheran	Roman Catholic	Episcopal	Pres/UCC/Chr	Meth/COCU
Isa. 52:13—53:12 or Hos. 6:1–6	Isa. 52:13—53:12	Isa. 52:13—53:12 or Gen. 22:1–18 or Wisd. 2:1, 12–24	Lam. 1:7–12	Isa. 52:13—53:12
Heb. 4:14–16; 5:7–9	Heb. 4:14–16; 5:7–9	Heb. 10:1–25	Heb. 10:4–18	Heb. 4:14–16; 5:7–9 or Heb. 10:1–25
John 18:1—19:42 or John 19:17–30	John 18:1—19:42	John (18:1–40) 19:1–37	Luke 23:33–46	John 18:1—19:42 or Luke 23:33–46

EXEGESIS

First Lesson: Isa. 52:13—53:12. For the remarks on this passage see above, pp. 34–36.

Second Lesson: Heb. 4:14–16; 5:7–9. For the third and last time in Holy Week, a text is taken from Hebrews which refers to Christ as High Priest. The repetition has been appropriate. The portrait of Jesus as great High Priest may not be unique to the author of the Epistle, but it is central to his thought. If for Paul that "name above every name" was the title "Lord," for the author of Hebrews it was "High Priest." Note, for example, the striking similarity in the rhythm or shape of the Christ hymn in Philippians 2 and Heb. 5:7–9. In the Christ hymn, Jesus,

> "though . . . in the form of God," took the "form of a servant . . .
> and being found in human form he . . . became obedient unto death.

> . . . Therefore God . . . highly exalted him and bestowed on him the name which is above every name."

In Hebrews 5, Jesus,

> "although he was a Son," nevertheless pursued a fleshly existence in which he "offered up prayers and supplications . . . was heard for his godly fear. . . . learned obedience through what he suffered," and was thus "made perfect . . . being designated by God a high priest after the order of Melchizedek."

Calling his readers to steadiness in the "race" by holding fast to their "confession," the Epistle writer thus fixes the community's certainty of a hearing at the "throne of grace," as well as the certainty of its "eternal salvation" in Jesus, that Son who for his obedience was "appointed" great High Priest (cf. 5:1–6).

What first meets the eye here is the text's strong affective coloration. More than one scholar has observed that here there is no "Pauline" refusal to know Christ "after the flesh," no Johannine penetration of every human attribute with the divine, but rather "a real incarnation." The observation is superficial. "High priest" is our author's catalyst, the concept which evokes the dialectic throbbing throughout the letter. "High priest" explains why our author can speak of Jesus' "flesh" as the "curtain" which hinders access to heaven (10:20), and as the entry into heaven itself (4:14; 9:11). "High priest" explains why Jesus can be described as "pioneer" (12:1), who in his own life achieved a full understanding of his community's "weakness" and thus its temptation to avoid suffering (4:15b; 5:7–8), and at the same time as "perfecter," who exercises his understanding of the community's plight in a "sympathizing with our weaknesses" (4:15a; 5:9). "High priest" explains why the Christian community can be portrayed as "wandering," running the "race" toward the "city which has foundations" (11:10), and at the same time as already in possession of its goal (12:22–24). "High priest" explains why faith and hope, or faith and "confidence" (4:16), are at bottom one and the same, since neither "faith" nor "hope" nor "confidence" is something one "has" as a subjective attitude, but is a straining toward something already given, the joyful choice of something already warranted by God. "High priest" is the concept which conjures up Jesus' earthly and historical past as well as his present and future, a concept forged in Judaism's dream of the ultimate union of the earthly and heavenly worlds but which now spells the truth that because God has shown himself to us "in these last days," the invisible future is already disclosed to us. And it is the "confession" of Jesus as "high priest," the "confession of our hope" (10:23), to which the community is called to "hold fast" (4:14).

In sum, "high priest" is the great "mediator" of Hebrews, and accounts for the use of all those alien categories of law and myth which finally comes round to exhausting their possibilities. And all of it drawn from what the Christian community already knew, already had at its elbow, all of it drawn from its own liturgy. The interpretive virtuosity of the author of Hebrews is as great as that of any other NT author.

Gospel: Luke 23:33–46. Nowhere in Luke's Gospel is the division between the believing and unbelieving within a single nation, the contest between the voluntary and involuntary, between human culpability and the divine decree, between the earthly, mundane, and the cosmic, transcendent, and finally, nowhere the interweaving of an individual's fate and that of his people pressed home with more intensity than in this evangelist's Good Friday scene.

On the one hand, that unidentifiable "they" bring Jesus to the place called The Skull. "They" crucify him. "They" cast lots to divide his garments. On the other, "the people" stand by watching. To the right and left of the victim hang two criminals, the one adding a third to the mockery of the rulers and Romans—"let him save himself!"—while the other gives lone testimony to Jesus' innocence and prays to be remembered. On the one hand a willful deed of execution, and on the other the acknowledgment of the perpetrators' ignorance: "They know not what they do." On the one hand rulers, soldiers as subject of the action, and on the other a death construed as submission to divine decree: "Father, into thy hands . . ." On the one hand an altogether earthly, natural-historical event—one more crucifixion, with all the political chicanery which served it as preface—and on the other a cosmic, transcendent event: "And there was darkness over the whole land until the ninth hour, while the sun's light failed, and the curtain of the temple was torn in two." On the one hand, a scoffing, mocking, and on the other a railing which spoke better than it knew: "The king of the Jews is *this one!*" God's exaltation of the crucified Jesus as prophet and servant like Moses, his enthronement of Jesus as royal Messiah and Son of David, is on the one hand a reproof of Israel and a demand for repentance, and on the other a gracious offer of forgiveness and life for Israel and the Gentiles: "Father, forgive them. . . . Truly, I say to you, today you will be with me in Paradise." This subtle interweaving in Luke's narrative sets him on a par with the ancient dramaturgists. References to Aeschylus or Sophocles are frequent in contemporary interpretations of Luke's passion. But it is precisely what he weaves which sets Luke apart from the literature of tragedy he had somehow come to know.

For years it has been assumed that Luke stood far enough from the actual events of Jesus' life to digest the raw, perplexing traditions in all their crudity, and make of them something less scandalous and more easily assimilable, with the result that there is no "theology of the cross" in the Third Gospel beyond the affirmation that the Christ "must" suffer, since so the Scriptures had foretold. The assumption is false. Luke's community was in crisis. It awaited the kingdom's coming and yet suffered persecution. The evangelist thus drew a portrait of Jesus that was calculated to assist his readers in coming to grips with their fate, the portrait of a Jesus whose destiny took its origin from his status as the Christ—"this one" had to suffer *because* he was the Christ! Luke's community thus had to regard its persecution as marking its fellowship with the One by whom God would judge the living and the dead. For if Jesus was the fulfillment of Scripture, the present time of Luke's community was also in God's hands—God's promises would be fulfilled. The tragedy of Jesus and the story of his suffering people were therefore not the result of an evil fate; they took place according to the will of God who would save. If Luke did not shape his record according to the ancient song in Isaiah, it was because the theme of the servant's humiliation and exaltation had gripped him with an original force. It was no accident that years later the symbol of the ox, sacrificial victim, should be applied to Luke and his Gospel, a motif so lodged in the primitive community's worship that it would serve another, anonymous writer "to the Hebrews" with the core of his gospel: "Surely he has borne our griefs . . ."

"Behold, my servant! The king of the Jews is *this one!*"

HOMILETICAL INTERPRETATION

The use of the fourth servant song for Good Friday is almost inevitable. No other portion of the OT seems so dramatically to describe the life and mission of Jesus as the church came to understand it. So on this day of suffering and death the song of the servant who somehow saves and redeems the guilty by his guiltless rejection and blameless suffering sets the liturgical and theological stage for and understanding of what will be described in the Gospel and what will be imaged for us in the movement of the Good Friday observances. There is, in this song, no answer as to how or even why the servant redeemed through suffering. There is only the recognition that the servant suffered patiently and that the suffering was redemptive. The suffering servant opens the mystery of redemptive suffering and offers a field in which to understand Jesus and the paradoxes of human existence.

In the Second Lesson the lectionary turns again to Hebrews and gives us the image of Jesus the High Priest. On this day it is impossible to suggest a priestly identity for Jesus without calling to mind the images of sacrifice, blood, immolation, and propitiatory death. Here the themes of yesterday's readings with their concern for the double meaning of sacrifice and the notion of redemptive suffering suggested by the First Lesson inevitably coalesce. Priests offer sacrifices, and the priestly Jesus offers himself. His sacrifice creates, as did the sacrifices of Moses' young men in Exodus, a community. The sacrifice of Jesus condenses the two kinds of sacrifice found in the Exodus passage from yesterday, in that it provides, via the Eucharist, a means for sharing with God and one another in a solemn fellowship. At the same time, it is a quintessential sacrifice of obedience to God in which Jesus gives himself up in obedience, even the obedience of death on the cross. This in its turn picks up a central theme of Luke, whose version of the crucifixion serves as our Gospel. As we shall see, for Luke, the linchpin of Jesus' salvific action is his faithful obedience.

Though all of these images cluster round the short Hebrews passage in association with the use of the title "high priest" on this day of the crucifixion, they are not the main theme the lesson itself picks up. This portion of Hebrews grasps the notion of priest as *mediator.* We are able to ask for and obtain mercy and the necessary power to fulfill our calling in life (grace) because Jesus is our mediator. This mediation is possible because he became one of us and endured all that we endure in this world of sin and death.

Hebrews is couched in Neoplatonic terms so that the problems of salvation are conceptualized as the problem of the reuniting of a broken connectedness between the pure, holy Divine and the stained, sinful world of human existence. In this framework the idea that God would come from his realm to ours was enough to suggest a reconnectedness. Once this connectedness was achieved, it would seem clear to the author of Hebrews that the power of the divine would be available to us, permitting us to overcome the powers of sin and death until our final reunion with God either at our death or the Parousia.

For those of us moderns for whom the Neoplatonic world view does not provide a viable hermeneutic, we are left still with the notions of incarnation, identification, and enduring. These are images and metaphors which overflow the Neoplatonic framework of Hebrews and touch us at a deeper level. In a mysterious manner, the Divine, the cause of all that is, that which metaphysicians have called "being itself" and before which human beings can only stand in dumbfounded awe—this God has, out of love for us, deigned to become one of us. He has emptied himself of power and privilege and has identified himself wholly with us. We are known, understood, and loved in our fear and sin and death-destined humanity. The sharing aspect of priesthood is now radicalized, and the notion of a mediator takes on a new meaning. The Priest came and offered himself as one of us and yet was not conquered by the worst that sin and death could do. If we are so loved that he would suffer what we suffer and if even that suffering could not conquer that love, then our situation is different than we had feared. It will be possible for us because Jesus has done it, and the power of love which sustained him he makes available to us. His is the mediation of divine love. This image of the enduring mediator comports perfectly with the Lucan account of Jesus' death on the cross.

Luke-Acts, which supplies our Gospel, is now well understood to have as two of its motifs a view of salvation history and a theory of faithfulness as a component of that history. Recapitulation was a favorite Greek way of understanding history, and Luke-Acts seems to adapt a form of this as its framework. Creation was a kind of covenant with all of humankind. History until Jesus was a story of human disobedience breaking covenant with God and suffering the consequences. After each fall, however, God would reinstitute a covenant with some portion of the human race. Each fall and recovenanting, however, found the segment of humanity included in the latest covenant to be smaller. This pattern continued until there was only a small, faithful eschatological remnant left—Jesus and his followers. Then the followers broke and fell in the face of his arrest. At that point the faithful remnant was down to one—Jesus alone kept obedient faith until death on the cross. As a consequence, God raised Jesus from the dead and began a reversal of the process which had been taking place until Good Friday and Easter. The mission of the church was to disseminate the good news of the new creation in Jesus Christ. Acts is the story of the beginning of the success of God's New Covenant which is expected eventually to embrace all of humankind again, at which time the Parousia will occur and the Kingdom of God will be established.

In the economy of salvation, obedience and faithfulness are crucial. The paradigm of Luke's theology comes at the annunciation. God initiates his final effort at salvation by approaching a young Hebrew girl with a preposterous message. She is frightened but responds in faithful obedience: "Let it be to me according to your word." Mary's obedience permits the eventual establishment of the new creation. Thus, in every case, God will initiate and humankind will have the option, as it has had throughout history, of responding obediently or disobediently. Luke's version of the crucifixion must be seen against this background in order for it to appear more than merely heroic or tragic. It was a cosmic drama in which the fate of creation rested upon the obedience of Jesus. This obedience which did not break faith with God but instead manifested God's ultimate purpose of love and creativity is tested and found sufficient at the moment of Jesus' death.

Luke's account places Jesus in an unbearable position. Jesus is derided with vitriolic anger by the same people who lauded him five days earlier as he entered Jerusalem on Palm Sunday. He is tempted from below by the crowd, from above by the sign proclaiming him to be the king of the Jews. The temptation once endured in the desert is raised to an unimaginable level. The tragic irony of the Palm Sunday adulation becomes apparent. The people believe they have been misled by Jesus and pour out on him the hatred bred of a thousand disappointments. In fact, they have been misled only by their own anger. They wanted a Messiah of earthly power to drive out the hated Romans. Since Jesus has not fulfilled their expectation, they have made a terrible alliance with those same Romans to kill him. So the final crisis in history is cast in terms of tragic irony.

In the fourteen verses which comprise our Gospel, this Jesus' loving obedience and faith appear in three symbolic forms. First, as he is being reviled by those who are crucifying him, he speaks an intercessory word of forgiveness for them: "Father, forgive them; for they know not what they do."

Luke was a Gentile whose understanding of reality was rooted in Greek culture. The Hellenistic understanding of law was different from the Hebrew. The Greeks' law was the inexorable cosmic force by which every moral act had its implications and repercussions. The tragic Greek notion of hubris was not the Hebrew concept of disobedience but was rather a fatal flaw, a "blind spot" in an otherwise good person which caused that person to break taboo or a natural law. Though we might sympathize with such a person, we know if we are Greek that the consequences of that deed must work themselves out until a cosmic homeostasis is restored. Tragedy is borne with the Greek understanding that good people who break laws unwittingly must nevertheless suffer the consequences of their actions. In his first word from the cross, Luke has Jesus contravene this law. Though they did not know what they were doing, the people, that is, we, who crucified Jesus should have suffered for their deed. Jesus changes this heretofore unremitting law of nature, for he speaks as the Divine One who is also the victim of the hubris. "Father, forgive them for they know not what they do" changes the Greek understanding of reality in a radical way. Henceforth we need not suffer the effects of the sins our forebears, or even we ourselves, unwittingly commit.

Jesus' second word from the cross is to the thief on Jesus' side. He, unlike the crowd, knows what he has done and presumably also when he did it. At this point, however, he acknowledges his situation and admits the justice of his punishment. At the same time he recognizes, at least implicitly, the utter blamelessness of Jesus. It is not full-blown repentance, but it is an acknowledgment of sin. Symbolically, then, Jesus moves from those who do not know what they are doing to one who did know what he was doing and was, therefore, without any excuse. This man too is forgiven in the sense that he too is granted a future in the new creation. If the sin of the crowd is Greek, then the sin of the thief is Jewish. He is suffering for having willfully disobeyed the commandment against stealing. Now both Jew and Greek, that is, all people, are forgiven in terms of their own understanding of sin. Forgiveness here means that they are granted a future. Despite what they have done and caused, wittingly or unwittingly, all people are given the opportunity to respond anew to God's initiative. From this moment on, all people will have the option to be included in the new creation.

Yet it remains for the last word from the cross to be spoken. The cosmic significance of this moment is set carefully. The earth is covered in a pall of darkness, and the veil of the temple, symbol of the Old Covenant, is rent in two. Jesus cries with a loud voice in a final display of utter agony, and then as he dies he says, "Father, into thy hands I commit my spirit!" The victory is won, for Jesus has remained obedient and faithful to death. Unlike Mark's Jesus, Luke's does not ask why God has forsaken him. He has the faith which will permit his resurrection and the establishment of the new creation. The image is that in his final act of faith and obedience, Jesus "gives up," that is, offers up to God, his very life, and in so doing is joined back to God in an obedient harmony which will serve as the basis of the rebirth of all creation. In this Jesus is manifested as our Lord in the fullest sense of the word. What we could not and cannot do, he has done and does. He perseveres in loving obedience to God and so can grant to us forgiveness. In turning to him we find that we are given a future. The things we have done or left undone, the things we have inherited, which have been done to us, all those things done knowingly and unknowingly through Jesus are put away. We are, through his loving obedience, offered a part in the age to come and an opportunity to participate in that age now if we will respond to him in faithful obedience.

Thus the irony of Palm Sunday turns back upon itself, and the very sins which seemed to be the means of defeat for love become the instruments of salvation. The misunderstanding and anger of the people, the cynical political machinations of the Sanhedrin and Pilate, the cruelty of the soldiers and obscenity of a painful, public execution are transformed by faithful love into the very sources of forgiveness and new life. The most awful moment of death is the source of new birth. Easter is born in the death of Jesus.